Arnold Davis

His Mor...

Foraw

A State of Affairs

Across the Bridge

A the B.
New Stories

Gallant's Preface to Selected Stories

p. 37 "The inescapable loneliness of growing old."

Irving Layton

Varieties of Exile

From *Paris Notebooks* — given to Sandra Berry as gift

178-9

There is no such thing as a writer who has escaped being influenced.... (For "influences" I would be inclined to substitute "acquisitions". ....) WB

Style cannot be copied except by the untalented. It is, finally, the distillation of a lifetime of reading and listening, of selection and rejection.

PETER LANG
New York • Washington, D.C./Baltimore • Bern
Frankfurt am Main • Berlin • Brussels • Vienna • Oxford

Varieties of Exile

New Essays on Mavis Gallant

EDITED BY

Nicole Côté and Peter Sabor

PETER LANG
New York • Washington, D.C./Baltimore • Bern
Frankfurt am Main • Berlin • Brussels • Vienna • Oxford

Library of Congress Cataloging-in-Publication Data

Varieties of exile: new essays on Mavis Gallant /
[edited by] Nicole Côté and Peter Sabor.
p. cm.
Based on presentations at a symposium
held in Paris on Mar. 19, 1999.
Text in English and French.
Includes bibliographical references (p.) and index.
1. Gallant, Mavis—Criticism and interpretation. 2. Women and literature—
Canada—History—20th century. 3. Alienation (Social psychology) in literature.
4. Exiles in literature. I. Côté., Nicole. II. Sabor, Peter.
PR9199.3.G26 Z95 813'.54—dc21 2002021413
ISBN 0-8204-5693-4

Die Deutsche Bibliothek-CIP-Einheitsaufnahme

Varieties of exile: new essays on Mavis Gallant /
ed. by: Nicole Côté and Peter Sabor.
–New York; Washington, D.C./Baltimore; Bern;
Frankfurt am Main; Berlin; Brussels; Vienna; Oxford: Lang.
ISBN 0-8204-5693-4

Cover photo by Danielle Schaub

The paper in this book meets the guidelines for permanence and durability
of the Committee on Production Guidelines for Book Longevity
of the Council of Library Resources.

Printed in the United States of America

1999.

Table of Contents

Acknowledgments

We would like to thank the following people and institutions for their involvement in the publication of this volume of essays: Sophie Grandmagnac of the Canadian Cultural Centre in Paris, the Social Sciences and Humanities Research Council of Canada, Université Laval, Ellen Chapco, Troni Grande, Paul Hartman, Gisèle Lalonde, Marie Legroulx, Linda Morin, Heather Munro, Garry Sherbert, with special thanks to Sylvain Rheault. We are grateful to Danielle Schaub for graciously providing the picture of Mavis Gallant. We also acknowledge the generous contribution of the University of Regina to this project.

Introduction

Nicole Côté

The writings assembled in this book originated in the Mavis Gallant symposium—Varieties of Exile: A Symposium on the Writings of Mavis Gallant / Des variétés d'exil: un symposium sur l'oeuvre de Mavis Gallant—held in Paris on March 19, 1999. Peter Sabor, Professor of English at Université Laval (Quebec City), had proposed to the head of the CRELIQ (Centre de recherche en Littérature québécoise), Denis Saint-Jacques, a colloquium in honour of Mavis Gallant, a surprisingly little-known writer in her native province, Quebec. Readers might know that Mavis Gallant is Canadian, but they rarely are aware that she was born and lived most of her childhood in Montreal, changing languages with schools as others change coats. Mavis Gallant, known in English Canada as one of the finest short story writers of her generation, in the United States through the publication, as early as the fifties, of her short stories in the prestigious *New Yorker*, and in France through the translation of her works, was at last to be claimed, at least partially, by the Québec literary establishment.

As for Gallant herself, she makes no mystery of her Canadian origins, notwithstanding her preoccupation with various exiles, be they geographical, language or culture related. Gallant's fiction deals with characters in exile from, if not happiness, then fulfilment. The emphasis on the negative condition of exile in Gallant criticism reflects her pungent satire and her subtle, but sometimes bewildering, irony, her satire dealing mostly with the exile of characters from their own romantic vision of reality. Gallant's characters have a tendency to cope with reality by superimposing on it patterns which restrict their capacity to perceive it appropriately. In other words, they put these constraints on reality to make it fit their own obsolete, and thus inadequate, constructions. While these patterns may allow them to shield temporarily a loss in a process of mourning, they often become pernicious when the characters do not have the strength to shake them off or modify them.

As E.D. Blodgett reminds us, we might take as a hint pointing to Gallant's own work a characteristic that she attributed to the art of Marguerite Yourcenar (*Paris Notebooks*: 180–81), namely that her "subject is not cruelty, but heresy." Heresy being "a movement away from the official view in such a way as to promote division" (Blodgett, "Heresy": 4), it bears much in common with exile [1]. Heretic in manifold ways, "Gallant's texts [...] are continual alibis that forever gloss the official account into a condition of irony, playfully shifting and displacing meanings until the shambles constitutes its own economy and polis" (*idem*:5).

This heretical way of looking at the world is linked to irony and exile in that irony offers an experience of exile by giving a feeling of otherness, by providing a different outlook on oneself and the world. As Paul de Man puts it, irony lies in the discontinuity between sign and meaning, where the "sign points to something that differs from its literal meaning and has for its function the thematisation of this difference" (*Blindness*: 209).

Irony, an awareness of the difference between the assumed reality and an idealized or distorted version of it, whether experienced by the character or by the reader, produces the same intense feeling of exile from the meaning of things. The reader faced with irony must attempt to bridge the discontinuity between sign and meaning. In order to relieve the well-known discomfort created by the incomplete grasp of the meaning in Gallant's fiction, the reader endeavours to make sense—be it only tentative—and reach out from his or her own experience and knowledge.

The reader's grasp of irony in Gallant's stories is not to be taken as a final epiphany, an ultimate unveiling of truth, since it is never to be considered as an end where characters could reside secure in their final knowledge, no matter how alienating that knowledge may be. Memory, as a locus of the interplay between the "objective" past and what is perceived as important by a subjectivity, plays an important role in the characters' reorganization of the past. For Gallant then, memory's relation to a historical event is essentially ironic. As Paul de Man states, "irony becomes increasingly conscious of itself in the course of demonstrating the impossibility of our being historical" (*Blindness*: 211). The impossibility of reaching a vantage point in time where one could judge history is precisely what Gallant points to when debunking the myth of an objective, transparent history. Thus she has created a certain number of characters—contrary to other, more felicitous ones, whose happiness lies in oblivion—who have the ability to attempt a subjective reconstruction of the past and to recognize that they must take responsibility for their unavoidably partial rebuilding of history.

For Blanchot, nevertheless, "Speech [...] is the promised land where exile fulfills itself in sojourn since it is not a matter of being at home there but of being always Outside, engaged in a movement wherein the Foreign offers itself, yet without disavowing itself" (*Infinite Conversation 128*). This is precisely what is at play in Gallant's fiction, where language points to meaning as a horizon, to be reached for, yet never attained. If, for the most part, Gallant's irony feels to the reader more like an affliction than a pleasure of the text, it may be because, in Blanchot's phrase, "Affliction is the loss of a dwelling place" (*Infinite Conversation* 122). Gallant's irony engages the reader in a paradoxical movement of exile that keeps the promise of reaching home by denying it.[2] This might also be a metaphor for the narrative: what is a story but the postponing of the resolution until the end, where the story will cease to exist?

One could examine a last variety of exile in the context of the colloquium on Mavis Gallant: the translation of her works, which Gallant has always considered problematic. Hers might appear as a paradoxical position, since she was raised in a bilingual environment. Nonetheless, this stance might very well spring from an acute awareness of the linguistic and cultural gulf between the French and English communities as she knew them in the Montreal of her childhood.

As impossible as literary translation appears to be, it is necessary, for: "A text [...] lives on only if it is at once translatable and untranslatable. Totally translatable, it disappears as a text, as writing, as a body of language. Totally untranslatable [...], it dies immediately" (Derrida, *Living On*: 102).[3] The displacement of meaning, amongst other things, can be seen as unavoidable in literary translation, since meaning is uprooted from its original language: the very singularity of the English idiom (or any other, for that matter)—in which Gallant's is rooted—while calling for a translation, always resists it.

" [...] Literature [...] is indissociably linked to idiom, to the corpora of natural languages" , says Derrida (*A Taste*: 11) .The translator is thus, like the characters in the short story, always "going ashore", trying to reach the shores of a solid continent of meaning, a definite interpretation. Blanchot's metaphor of speech as a promised land can also be applied to translation, since translation is doubly "a promised land where exile fulfills itself in sojourn": as a no man's land (or sea) between two languages that necessarily do not coincide; as a wandering from a fixed meaning and towards a horizon, the nature of which is unattainable, since it recedes as one advances.

Danielle Schaub's "Mavis Gallant's Irony and its Destabilizing Double Edge: Translating the Exile's Experience" makes obvious this subtle link between irony and exile by presenting irony as a marker of exile, whether it be in Gallant's themes, structure, syntax or narratorial instance. Schaub considers the cultural conditions that brought about Mavis Gallant's dual outlook on life, examining the resulting tension between "certainty and uncertainty, intention and actualization, utterance and silence" [...], "translating the instability and disconnectedness of the exile's experience" (14). Gallant's indirection and allusion "presuppose the reader's ability to decipher" (15), the reader's reaction often echoing the protagonist's bewilderment and frustration "when confronted with the indeterminate gaps of a narrative" (21). Examining three stories, "The Other Paris," "Potter" and "His Mother," Schaub investigates the thematic and structural links between irony and exile. In "The Other Paris", Schaub explores the double exile—geographical and emotional— of Carol Frazier, and Gallant's constant stressing of the gaps between Carol's imagined Paris and the real one, leading her life to an impasse. Schaub convincingly argues that Gallant's workings of irony in structural devices are as precise as her syntax —hence, the "statements that do not connect smoothly" (16), the abrupt changes of registers, the omniscient narrator's use of juxtaposition, whereas Carol's statements are coordinated, as if the protagonist could weave a matrix around a core of emotional chaos. Irony resides also in the very plot: "to discover her self-imposed exclusion, the reader has to follow Carol in her meanderings through Paris and in the text's complicated intersection of past and present" (19). Schaub even highlights a seemingly innocent detail like a typographical device: a space isolating the seminal scene of the concert, where, along with the ceiling, Carol's hopes of knowing the real Paris and true love crumble. Through this careful thematic and formal analysis of "The Other Paris," Schaub shows how preconceived ideas are lethal to Gallantian characters, who superimpose them on reality instead of acknowledging the unforeseen.

In her study of "Potter," Schaub shows how ridiculous traits in the protagonists further compromise their unstable position. Laurie Bennett's mispronunciation of her lover's name—Peter, Potter, Porter, Otter, for Piotr—points both to Laurie's intellectual and cultural limitations and to the various roles she attributes to him. Piotr's love of Laurie, despite her ludicrous ignorance, stems from her ability to open up "new horizons, making him feel some forthcoming connection" (28).

In her analysis of a third story, "His Mother," Schaub conveys the workings of Gallantian irony by contrasting the said and the unsaid "underlying most parent/child conversation" (30) and the mother's "anguished need of recognition and aimlessness owing to her lost role in her son's life. An emotional pauper, she stands on the shaky grounds of outsiders" (31). As Schaub specifies, Gallant's "short stories and novellas present in semi-serious tone the aberrations of the system in which, or by which, her characters live, turning them all into exiles of sorts" (31–32).

Janice Kulyk Keefer's "'Radiant Paradigms and Chinks of Light:' Mavis Gallant's Polish Émigrés in Paris" is an elegiac reflection on Gallant's deeply ethical work. Analysing two linking stories, "Forain" and "A State of Affairs", she discusses the moral issues raised by the characters of aging Polish émigrés (Tremski, Wroblewski) and their wives (Barbara, Magda) as well as of their Parisian publisher, Blaise Forain. Between their post-War arrival and post-Wall old age, half a century has gone by and brought about Western values. Yet the stories are not so much about the former clash of Western and Eastern ideologies maintaining these Polish writers in anonymity as they are about the change from a manichean system of beliefs to that of a single, global, amnesic culture based on market economy.

Keefer notes how the stories offer complementary perspectives, "from the point of view of Blaise Forain, a dubious Parisian publisher of Eastern European literature in translation" (37–38) to that of Mr Wroblenski in "A

State of Affairs," "as problematic a focalizer as Blaise Forain" (38), because of his unreliable memory and perceptions, blighted by old age. As Keefer is quick to point out, the stories present disturbing parallels: Forain and his ambivalent motives are matched by Carole Fournier, the bank official, who, though benign, "offers and then withdraws a vital service" (39) to Mr Wroblewski. Her generation, information-laden, is pitted against the old and the old world, clinging to memory. The unwilling amnesia of Magda is paralleled by the willing forgetfulness of Halina, as well as by that of the younger generation, which seems content to live without the background of collective memory. In the same vein, suggests Keefer, Mr Wroblewski's unnamed old friend, with his formidable memory and his capacity to provide a context for every event, offers an interesting contrast to journalists whose partial digging into history is a function of their immediate needs. Keefer presents as an antithesis to Fournier's computer screen the exchange of letters between Mr Wroblewski and his Jewish friend in Warsaw and the letters Magda writes after forty-five years of delay. Keefer thus highlights the opposition between a nostalgic view of a nearly extinct generation and a "succinct, caustic view of the new, post-Wall generation," come to Paris to lead "more materially rewarding lives" (39).

Because of their fleeting lives and their clinging to the past, the old Polish émigrés come to stand as memory itself, unreliable yet indispensable for the insight they bring to modern life. Objects of their past become the mnemonic artefacts of a long-vanished era, in the same way as the Berlin Wall stood as a "radiant paradigm" to Wroblewski. In a kind of postface to her essay, Keefer examines the imagery of light and darkness in the two short stories and thus opposes the "suspect glitter of the city's lights" (47) to the darkness of the immigrants' lives and the bleaker darkness of racism.

Agnès Whitfield's "Displaying Differ*a*nce: 'Across the Bridge' by Mavis Gallant" examines deferral on the levels of narrative tone, theme, plot and meaning, using two of Gallant's texts: "Across the Bridge" and Gallant's preface to her *Selected Stories*. Whitfield's goal is here to highlight the processes at work in the author's aesthetics of writing, whether it be fictional or partly autobiographical.

Whitfield introduces her hypothesis by explaining that Derrida's concept of *différance* is rooted in time (to defer or temporise) as well as in space (displacement). With Gallant, meaning is never given, but left to be interpreted, through a variety of deferral techniques. Gallant's narrative tone necessarily involves a deferral of meaning, since the reader, as Whitfield notes with Smythe, is "involved in a complex process of 'transferential reconstruction' " (Whitfield, 50, quoting Smythe, 29). Another aspect of this deferral is that Gallant chooses to look at an emotional crisis from the point of view of its aftermath. The characters are shown to be quite unable to interpret what has happened, which leads them to "displaced repetition" (Whitfield, 50), implying "subtle alteration, variations within each repetition" (Besner quoted by Whitfield, 51).

Gallant's characters themselves are foreigners, that is, *displaced*, or feeling so. Whitfield points out Gallant's paradoxical statements about the necessity to maintain a tight border between the two languages while keeping silent about the invisible translations in her stories (French characters speaking English). According to Whitfield, Gallant uses "similar tropes to portray her contradictory position vis-à-vis language and difference in her preface to the collection of stories and in her story 'Across the Bridge' " (53). The bridge is used by Gallant as a displaced trope of the unknown awaiting on the other shore, "desired perhaps yet necessarily deferred" (*idem*). Since "Across the Bridge" has to do with a wedding, it should symbolize a bridging of differences. But, as Whitfield contends, "the theme of marriage is, from the very beginning, set against the [...] perhaps unbridgeable inequality in language and power which underlies difference between men and women" (54). Though the plot has the protagonist cross the bridge twice, the crossing itself is obliterated on both occasions.

Strangely, contends Whitfield, "the same tropes of bridge, river, banks, sky, writing and painting, as well as their symbolic evocations of displacement and deferral, reappear in the author's autobiographical preface to her *Selected Stories*" (57). Whitfield shows how "structurally the spatial configuration of the autobiographical narrative of Mavis Gallant's second trip home [...] is almost identical with Sylvie's aborted crossing of the Seine, and equally ambiguous" (58). In both texts, the trope of the bridge is used to represent the crossing from one language to another (each associated with a parent). Nevertheless, "the act of crossing is alluded to, yet not represented, endlessly deferred [...]" (59). Each language is shown in both texts as "literally and symbolically wanting," with neither of the two parental languages to be embraced totally. Nonetheless, "both texts situate access to language as a form of artistic expression [...] between the two shores of difference" (60).

Marta Dvorak's "Mavis Gallant's Fiction: Taking the (Rhetorical) Measure of the Turning Point" shows, in her detailed textual analysis, how much the rhetorical devices, that is, the form, contribute to meaning. Gallant's prose, with its "disparate components, [...] yoking of abstract, concrete, sensory, affective and intellectual elements" (63) is, according to Dvorak, pointillist in manner and phenomenological in its approach, "capturing with small touches fragments of perception, bits of reality" (63).

The "confused colliding of sensations, impressions and experiences" (Van Gunsteren, 55, quoted by Dvorak, 64) proper to literary impressionism is produced through accumulation and concatenation, painting "clusters of images" (64) Gallant's texts, "non-linear, multilayered, multidimensional, multi-genre constructions" (64), involving several temporal dimensions, are further complicated by their usual ironic mode. In that respect, Dvorak, by linking Barthes' definition of literature—"La première condition de la littérature, c'est, paradoxalement, d'accomplir un langage indirect: nommer en détail les choses afin de ne pas nommer leur sens dernier" (65)—shows two things: first, that all literature is ironic in essence (as Frye said); second, that Gallant's works are supremely ironic, since her "'clusters of images', like the irony, serve in an indirect fashion to designate a second meaning" by "displacement or disjunction" (65).

Dvorak is also very attentive to Gallant's syntax as yet another means of carving out meaning through form; for instance, "the paratactic erasure of a discursive segment, " in "Orphans' Progress," "reflects visually [...] the rubbing out of the relationship with the mother" (66). Enumeration as an exemplum in the passage dealing with the goat conveys, rather than explains, the little sisters' feelings of "terror, powerlessness, and alienation" (67). As well, in other parts of the short story, polysyndetons and anaphors, endowing the syntax with a hypnotic quality, contrast "the plenitude and power of the girls' former position as subjects when living with their mother (*they knew*), with the notion of absence and their status of powerless objects, empty receptacles to be filled with imparted (and therefore biased or questionable) information (*until told/ until they were told*)" (69). Metaphor is also a Gallantian device which "generates double vision", allowing "the reader to see one thing under the aspect of another" (69).

Other rhetorical devices used by Gallant that permit "strategies of displacement" (72) include hypallage which, by fusing the qualifier and the qualified, jolts "the reader into seeing with the fresh vision of a child" (72). Zeugma, "an atypical yoking of disparate elements, often an abstract and a concrete one" (72), can exacerbate the ridiculous in a romantic vision of the world: in "Varieties of Exile," the narrator's "a man *with no prospects and no teeth in his head*" (quoted by Dvorak, 73), poking fun at Frank Cairns' idealizing of poverty, forces the reader to suspect clichés and revisit seeming truths. As Dvorak reminds us, Gallant's texts "are both cipher and hermeneutic instruments with which to read and interpret the cipher of the world" (73).

The roundtable on translation that followed the papers (summarized here since it has been transcribed in its original French) turned out to be as much about the idiosyncrasies of Mavis Gallant's style, themes, voice, tone and manner as it was about issues of translation. Pierre-Edmond Robert and Geneviève Doze, being Parisians, had the advantage of knowing her work "from the inside." Pierre-Edmond Robert was interested in translating Gallant because, as a reader of the *New Yorker*, he had read her short fiction about Paris while in the United States. A professor and a well-known Proust critic, Robert presents translation as a critical work: "In fact, what I felt like saying about Mavis's work, I said in my translations, instead of in a critical work" (80–81; translation mine). Robert nonetheless compares the act of translation to a balance sheet, a statement of accounts, where everything which was in the left column must find its way into the right. Perhaps because this calls for a perfect transcription of content—which, in literature, is illusory— Robert explains that in order to reach that balance, one must upset "many things" within the form. Compelled to choose between words, of which none is perfect, the translator, says Robert, will need to resort to artifice.

According to Geneviève Doze—who is also Alice Munro's translator—empathy, the desire to get into the characters and the author's skin, is the prime factor in a good translation. Nonetheless, she confesses to having had difficulties making her way into the syntax: her French translation, she found (a translator's humility at work, for she is indeed a wonderful translator), was invariably too heavy for the incisiveness, the sharpness of Gallant's expression.

Agnès Whitfield mentions her interest in the fact that Gallant's French stories are in English as if the characters were living in France but somehow dwelled in the English language—whereas in the translation, the characters paradoxically express themselves in their native language. Later, Gallant explains that she is very careful in creating French characters, and that it is only after a very long experience of French life that she came to create French characters observing strangers or themselves.

Jane Koustas speaks of Gallant's representation of difference in her short stories and of her reception in France. The French, often searching Canada's identity through its novelists, had to revert to style with Gallant, since one cannot read Gallant in order to know only Canada.

Doze sees Gallant's Canadian gaze on French society as that of an ethnologist's. "It is", adds Robert, "the privilege of someone who knows very well French reality, using all the while a reference system outside of it" (84; translation mine). Contrary to this tradition of Anglophone writers exiled in Paris, living with an expatriate crowd, Gallant, continues Robert, evokes the quintessential French reality, devoid of all the usual clichés proper to Anglo-Americans.

Gallant being bilingual, the collaboration between the translators and the author has been fruitful. Since translators cannot always see their work from a distance, asserts Doze, she was grateful for Gallant's interventions. Robert, regarding the difficulties of translating Gallant's style, insists on the importance of rendering French tone, music and rhythm—and since the rhythm of French has little to do with that of English, that it should at least echo the original. Robert endorses a movement away from the style of English in order to preserve the elusive qualities of Gallant's prose.

The Questions and Answers session—which had begun before the end of the roundtable, everyone being eager to hear Mavis Gallant—leaves the last word to the author. Comments on both sides revolved around the origin of fiction and the role of criticism.

Gallant's relationship to criticism, especially the theoretical aspect of it, is one of skepticism:

> But the raw material of fiction has come from another source, so that criticism is almost impossible for the author to follow [...] For serious critics, the problem is that no matter how much is revealed in the text, the sources of fiction remain invisible. (108)

To Gallant, the image is the kernel of a story. With Marta Dvorak, Gallant explored the birth of a story: the image coming from nowhere, people in a frozen situation, then getting in motion, each coming alive with a precise voice, accent, vocabulary.

The critics, Gallant says, need to find "the element that shaped the image for the writer" (109). Nevertheless, they can only look at a work from the outside of what she calls "the glass house of fiction" (112), evoking the invisible barrier between creator and writer. Jacques Leclaire's belief that, in the best of cases, the critic is in the position of the conductor, giving one interpretation of the work, is a satisfying point of view for a critic, who knows that however incomplete the interpretation is, it still has the merit of providing an access to the work. This metaphor of the conductor/music interpreter has been used repeatedly by theoreticians of translation, translation and criticism being considered as derivative and interpretative; yet they remain, like music interpretation, unmistakably creative. Nonetheless, says Gallant, to be on both sides—interpretation and creation—at the same time is not for her: should she choose to write *and* interpret her work, her fiction would be lost: "Si je commençais à écrire de cette façon, ce serait illisible" (115).

Notes

1. A situation a Canadian can understand particularly well, according to Blodgett: "A Canadian is, it would seem, [...] thus endowed with attributes similar to those of a woman in a patriarchal world" (Blodgett,"Heresy'': 5).
2. A number of ideas in this introduction have been developed in a collaborative project with Dr Garry Sherbert. I thank him for generously contributing his ideas to this paper, particularly for pointing me to writers like Blanchot for the link between exile and the promise land, and Derrida, for presenting one's mother tongue as already a foreign tongue in that it is shaped and inhabited by others before one and with one.
3. This idea was first presented by Walter Benjamin in his famous essay "The Task of the Translator".

Mavis Gallant's Irony and its Destabilizing Double Edge

Translating the Exile's Experience

Danielle Schaub

Years ago, when I first started reading Mavis Gallant's oeuvre, I was attracted by her multiple pictures of the exile's experience. Having myself been displaced by force and then by choice more than once, I found a reflection of my own perceptions in her stories and decided to focus my doctoral research on her short fiction. Little did I know then how much I would gain from that decision. Only later when I was preparing myself for my defence did I understand the profound impact Gallant had left on me. While I was summing up the results of my research, I was hit by the realization that the pleasure I had derived from my critical approach of her texts went far beyond her writing. True I had learnt substantially about her perfected techniques and enjoyed decoding and discussing them, but I had overlooked the wisdom she had imparted to me. Her acute perception of the world and its inhabitants has indeed made me look at them from a different, more interesting angle. I believe we are all here to celebrate Mavis Gallant, the grandeur of her vision and her masterly compositions. I for one would like to pay special homage to her as a past master in irony. By sharing her outlook I have learned a great deal about life; she helped me face difficult circumstances by distancing myself from them, by decoding their hidden meaning without letting them cripple me emotionally. It should therefore surprise no one that I have chosen to speak about her irony and its translation of the exile's experience. Gallant's ironic perspective might well result from her experience of culture and language, based on diversity and heterogeneousness. Having been torn from her natural Anglo-Saxon Protestant background at the age of four to be raised in a French Catholic convent school and subsequently sent to numerous schools according to the whims and the itinerant *trajet* of her mother, she has a composite vision of life. Looking at once through two lenses (French and British), she cannot have one, and only one, view of things. Her bilingual education indeed left her "with two systems of behavior, divided by syntax and tradition; two environments to consider, one becalmed in a long twilight of nineteenth-century religiosity; two codes of social behavior; much practical experience of the difference between a rule and a moral point" (*Selected Stories*, xv). The resulting awareness that whatever she saw, heard and said could be interpreted in two diametrically opposed manners led her to realize that she herself could not utter, let alone write, anything without having an ironic inner smile, mirroring the "other" position. Forever an exile on home grounds, she perceives culture and language as double; rooted in her upbringing, this understanding of their duality has resulted in disengagement, in a lightness of perception, making her look at things and people from a dispassionate, and therefore ironic, angle. Her having uprooted herself again at a later stage contributed to further estrangement, every new situation increasing the number of lenses through which she looks at people. Since she mingles with both locals and exiles wherever she lives, the perspective is constantly reduplicated. As a consequence, hers is "an irony that understands limitations and contradictions as often inevitable, and even necessary—and therefore eludes the negative connotations usually evoked by the term" (Siemerling, 132). This she emphasizes, in a way, by confiding that irony is "just a way of looking at things [...][My tone] is not laid on. It is the way I am, probably" (Hancock, 52). The conflicting juxtaposition of affirmation and hypothesis in the last sentence brilliantly exemplifies one of the manners in which the Gallantian tension between certainty and uncertainty, intention and actualization, utterance and silence manifests itself, translating the instability and disconnectedness of the exile's experience.

Inherent in her character, irony is one of the most discussed devices in Gallant's work. Though they do not dwell on it as a predominant trope of reading, and even less on its reproduction of the exile's insecure position, the earlier critiques already refer to it as "perhaps the most important technical element in any Gallant novel" (Godard, 73), and, one should add, or story. Barbara Godard rightly asserts that "at the centre of [her] literary concerns from her earliest writing has been a preoccupation with the tension between appearance and reality."[1] In addition, "indirection and allusion— two major elements in Gallant's writing—work out their own ironic patterns of revelation, sometimes counterpointing, sometimes heightening the irony that undermines assertions by recasting them as merely apparent certainties" (Besner, "Rereading, "3).[2] Irony, Siemerling adds, is also "linked to Gallant's view of the possibilities and impossibilities of human perception of the self and others, and to the role of memory in this process" (135–6).[3] Put differently, "her fiction pronounces no universal truths—it works by ironic indirection, by oblique angles of vision, and by the presentation of images in clouded mirrors" (Keefer, *Reading*, 21). This statement, like the preceding ones, presupposes the reader's ability to decipher. As with many of her techniques—polyphonic, spatial, structural, stylistic, to mention but a few—Gallant's irony affects the reception of her stories, forcing the reader's active participation to decode the dissociated layers of the text. But over and above its impact on reception, Gallant's twist admirably grasps the ill-groundedness of the exile's life. Forever conscious of the multiple facets of life, Gallant exposes the marginality of her characters' lives by ironic touches, somehow revealing their emotional, social or geographical estrangement.

In this respect, "The Other Paris" informs Gallant's writing most obviously and reveals how irony and the conflicting perspectives it usually involves convey the exile's experience.[4] Through twists and turns, the story discloses how Carol Frazier, a young educated American woman living in Paris, "set[s] about the business of falling in love" (*Other Paris*, 4) with her American boss, Howard Mitchell, who has proposed to her "over a tuna-fish salad" (3). She has learned "from helpful college lectures on marriage" that "a common interest, such as a liking for Irish setters, [is] the true basis for happiness, and that the illusion of love [is] a blight imposed by the film industry" (4). However, in spite of her pragmatism, she is convinced that the Parisian setting will provide the right emotions. Idealized to extremes, her vision of Paris is contrasted with her perception of the drabness around her, a perception she eventually sets out to forget and replaces by her idealized version, a decision guiding her romantic approach to love and marriage. In contrast to Carol's approach, Odile, the destitute French secretary of aristocratic origins, lives by real emotions. She supports her lover Felix, an unemployed refugee fifteen years younger than her. Her life drastically contradicts the message of the lectures Carol attended, according to which "similar economic backgrounds, financial security, belonging to the same church—these [are] pillars of the married union" (4). Even this bare plot summary suggests the irony contained in the story and the disharmonious pictures of life, translating Carol's inability to find her proper niche. Twice an exile, first by virtue of her geographical displacement, and second by virtue of the invented romantic setting as well as feelings for Howard, Carol cannot relate to anyone truly.

Grasping the tenuous grounds on which Carol's life is based, Gallant enhances the contrasts between Carol's dream life and reality from the very beginning:

> If anyone had asked Carol at what precise moment she fell in love, or where Howard Mitchell proposed to her, she would have imagined, quite sincerely, a scene that involved all at once the Seine, moonlight, barrows of violets, acacias in flower, and a confused, misty background of the Eiffel Tower and little crooked streets. This was what everyone expected, and she had nearly come to believe it herself. (3)

Gallant shows how Carol embarks on a track that will distance her from her reality. As an outsider, she forges her life according to the preconceived ideas she has inherited. Irony conveys Gallant's consciousness of the process and its corrective picture.

Even within the couple alienation prevails, as appears from Howard`s thoughts:

> He was touched by her shy good manners, her earnest college French. His friends liked her, and, more important, so did the wives of his friends. He had been seriously in love on earlier occasions, and did not consider it a reliable emotion. He and Carol got on well, which seemed to him a satisfactory beginning. (5–6)

Though less critical, the narrator emphasizes the lack of genuine feelings by juxtaposing statements that do not connect smoothly. Jumping from Howard's superficial feelings through his friends' appreciation and then from his past passions to his tolerant acceptance of the situation, the discourse sounds like an ironic counterpoint to Carol's college lectures. Allusions to the normal course of romantic development contribute further irony:

> His friends, however, told him that she was obviously in love with him and that it was pretty to see. This he expected, not because he was vain but because one took it for granted that love, like a harmless familiar, always attended young women in friendships of this nature. Certainly he was fond of Carol and concerned for her comfort. Had she complained of a toothache, he would have seen to it that she got to a dentist. (6)

Knowing how Carol feels, how she sets about to love Howard, the reader smiles while reading the first two sentences, for they reveal how romantic ideals colour the perception people have of Carol, whether they are implicated or not in the relationship; generated by the reader's active reading process, the ironic smile highlights the connections drawn. The abrupt transition to Howard's feelings and concern jumps back to the last sentence of the previous passage emphasizing contentment with the situation; but the next sentence hilariously reduces the romantic appeal, projecting it onto a different, more pragmatic plane. An awareness of the change in registers effected in this passage allows the reader to surmise that passion does not drive the new couple; estrangement governs their relations.

The narrative then displays a far more complicated course of relationship than at first assumed. Carol's dissatisfaction with her life goes back to allusions attributing her lack of love to the unromantic weather, to the as-yet-undiscovered true Paris, to the non-existent connections with French society. Originating in her awareness that she does not share anything with anyone, Carol's disappointment is disclosed every day when "thinking that an evening, a special kind of evening [is] forming all over the city, and that she ha[s] no part in it" (8). It is further silently voiced through questions and hypotheses interspersed in the text: "Where was the Paris she had read about? Where were the elegant and expensive-looking women? Where, above all, were the men, those men with their gay good looks and snatches of merry song, the delight of English lady novelists?" (6); "There must be more to it than this" (8). Thus here and there the fractured narrative implicitly insists on the absence of real emotional involvement from the start and a refusal to examine its implications as evidenced in the following revelatory passage: "Temporarily, she put the question of falling in love to one side. Paris was not the place, she thought; perhaps it had been, fifty years ago, or whenever it was that people wrote all the songs. It did not occur to her to break her engagement" (13). The reader has to make out from the previous jumble of statements—taking them in all directions—that Carol's present allusions to the picture of Paris in the famous love songs suggest her refusal to address its romantic, thus unreal nature, as well as inform the unsound grounds for her engagement.

Carol, it appears, does not want to see where the emotions lie, for fear of an unconventional plot. She may well think that "if she spoke to the right person, or opened the right door, or turned down an unexpected street, the city would reveal itself and she would fall in love" (9), but the minute she faces them, she rejects them as unsuitable because they do not correspond to the image of love and to the Paris imprinted in her mind. This definitely holds for Odile's friend, Felix, who puzzles Carol. The oxymoronic look on his face—"at once bold and withdrawn" (9)—engenders equally contradictory feelings in her—attraction and repulsion. Wondering about Felix's origins, Carol asks Howard what he knows about him. " 'Why are you so interested?' he said. But Carol was not interested" (10). While the reported answer amounts to brushing off the topic as irrelevant, the story nevertheless implies a link, however superficial, that ties Carol and Felix: "After that, Carol [sees] Felix every evening" (10), keeps registering his appearance, and discusses him with Odile—all signs of interest rather than indifference. Soon after Carol gleans information about Felix, the link appears stronger, even if contrived:

> That night, before going to sleep, she thought about Felix, and about how he was only twenty-one. She and Felix, then, were closer in age than he was to Odile or she herself was to Howard. When I was in school, he was in school, she thought. When the war stopped, we were fourteen and fifteen... But here she lost track, for where Carol had had a holiday, Felix's parents had been killed. Their closeness in age gave her unexpected comfort, as if someone in this disappointing city had some tie with her. (10–11)

This passage exposes the lie of Carol's previous claim to disinterest. Subsequent confrontations, nonetheless, disclose that Carol keeps denying Felix a real part in her life. Ignoring him or objecting to one or another aspect of his personality (11, 16, 19, 22, 24), she minimizes the impact of her encounters with him.

Carol's conscious decision to ignore Felix and attempts to enforce it expose another reality:

> In the morning she was ashamed of her disloyal thoughts—her closest tie in Paris was, after all, with Howard—and decided to ignore Felix when she saw him again. That night, when she passed his chair, he said 'Good evening,' and she was suddenly acutely conscious of every bit of her clothing: the press of the belt at her waist, the pinch of her earrings, the weight of her dress, even her gloves, which felt as scratchy as sacking. It was a disturbing feeling; she was not sure that she liked it. (11)

Carol obviously cultivates an illusion: once again, though one sentence expresses her claims to love Howard and to will Felix out of her sight, the next one turns to Felix and gives ample details of the physical stirs his presence elicits in her. The concluding statements of the passage signify Carol's blindness to those emotions that would lead her to experience love. The to-ing and fro-ing between the assumed pose and the real feelings nonetheless keeps unsettling the reader, who cannot advance any interpretation with certainty, for at any time the narrative shifts back to a previous set of data, negating the most recent ones.

Further instances of intense closeness and emotional excitement prove that Carol will ignore "the right person," "the right door," the turning into "an unexpected street." To discover her self-imposed exclusion, the reader has to follow Carol in her meanderings through Paris and in the text's complicated intersections of past and present. Carol's reaction when she sees Felix at a concert given by Martine, Odile's sister, informs the awkward wavering that pulls the reader along: "She felt a spasm of annoyance, and at the same time her heart began to beat so quickly that she felt its movement must surely be visible" (16). But she refuses to understand the emotions, or at least misinterprets them. For immediately after recording her heartbeats, she weighs their occurrence in a most confused manner:

> What ever is the matter with me, she thought. If one could believe all the arch stories on the subject, this was traditional for brides-to-be. Perhaps, at this unpromising moment, she had begun to fall in love. She turned in her seat and stared at Howard; he looked much as always. She settled back and began furnishing in her mind the apartment they would have in Chicago. (16)

Ironically Carol decodes her emotions correctly; she has begun to fall in love, but not with the man who fits her idealized picture of marriage. The contrast between her emotional reaction to Felix and her indifference to Howard becomes clearer as she sets out to forget the feelings by letting her pragmatic sense take over. After several oscillations between one and the other, the reader may eventually attribute her attitude to a fight between conventionalism and nonconformism.

Such an interpretation may have been facilitated by a typographical device singling out a scene: halfway through the story the concert attracts the reader's attention by virtue of its highlighted position between blank spaces before and after. On the one hand, the initial space might correspond to the break necessitated by the reader's pondering over the three sentences Carol writes in a letter to her parents to mention the concert. Whereas the prospective event kindles her imagination and stirs up her excitement, Carol's correspondence tones down emotions to the point of suppressing them altogether. Since she privileges surface smoothness over deep feelings, she makes sure that her letters "sound properly casual" (15). Unreproduced, the letters set readers' minds at work; the degree of indeterminacy caused by the unwritten forces them to picture the content of the letters. As the latter "ha[ve] not contained much of interest" (15), the reader visualizes a jumble of irrelevancies interspersed with hints at another world, a reflection of her life in Paris.[5] On the other hand, the blank announcing the scene might signify the crucial value of the experience. Carol is convinced that the concert will introduce her into French society; yet the event itself is dismal, set in "an ordinary, shabby theatre" on "an obscure street" and the audience turns out "odd and shabby" (15, 17). The scene would then serve to contrast with her ideals, setting the glamourous picture of French society against its drab reality, and by extension the passionate love stories associated with Paris against the emotionless landscape she has visited.

The concert certainly causes a drastic change in Carol's approach: "For Carol, the concert was the end, the final *clou*. She stopped caring about Paris, or Odile, or her feelings for Howard" (20). Having witnessed the disdain of Odile's family for outsiders, Carol articulates her discontent and consciously erases any previous concern of hers. Her dissatisfaction also stems from Felix's catch phrase describing the attitude of Odile's family—"No admission for us foreigners" (19). The suggested lack of discrimination between Felix and herself vexes Carol: "it was even less kind of them to include [her] in a single category of foreigners. Surely Odile could see the difference between Carol and this pale young man who 'did other things'. She felt that she and Felix had been linked together in a disagreeable way, and that she was floating away from everything familiar and safe" (19). Carol's frustration curiously echoes the reader's feeling when confronted with the indeterminate gaps of a narrative that puts together so many apparently disparate elements.

As if the indeterminacies did not suffice to fragment the reader's perception of both characters and events, halfway through the story the narrative unexpectedly resumes the first scene. Aggravating the fracture, the disruption of chronology severs the tenuous thread from which the reader was suspended. Odile's reference to her nastiness at Madame Germaine's indeed directs the reader back to a long-forgotten scene interrupted by the description of Carol's life after her engagement. Only then do readers realize that Gallant has led them astray; the comparison between the illusory scene Carol would picture and the actual proposal has led to retrospective narration. Astutely concealing the anachronic nature of the information through successive speedy developments, Gallant distorts the reader's sense of chronology. Her cutting technique calls to mind the conceptually similar devices used to great effect in the montage of such films as *Rashomon*. Having cut her story into several parts, changed their natural order, and spliced everything together again, Gallant forces the reader to reconstruct the important scene at the dressmaker's in the light of the anachronisms.

The drastic break in the narration allows the reader to weigh Carol's approach to Odile's irony and to Felix's marginality in different terms. Indeed in the aftermath of the highlighted scene, Carol disconnects herself from her previous concerns. The change presumably helps the reader understand why "Odile's slight irony was perplexing" in the first section of the story at the dressmaker's, the more so as the account reiterates people's assumptions concerning Carol's engagement:

> Everyone seemed to think it normal that now her only preoccupation should be the cut of her wedding dress. People began giving parties for her. The wash of attention soothed her fears. She was good-tempered, and did not ask Howard to take her to tiresome places. Once again he felt he had made the right decision, and

> put her temporary waywardness down to nerves. After a while, Carol began lunching with Odile again, but she did not mention the concert. (20)

Justifying Carol's lack of insight, the passage alternates standpoints, which thrusts the reader in all sorts of directions because of their allusive character. While the first sentence reflects Carol's innocent outlook on the decisions made at the dressmaker's, thus precluding any irony and begging the reader as it were to share her perspective, the second and third jump by mere narratorial allusions to completely different aspects of the period, left to the reader to connect and visualize; furthermore the reference to Carol's fears evokes her lack of love for Howard and her suppressed emotions for Felix while calling to mind her desperate attempts to enter French society so as to fall in love. The fourth sentence curiously combines the narrator's, Carol's, and Howard's approaches: the use of the adjectives "good-tempered" and "tiresome" has different values depending on the angle of vision the reader decides to share. They definitely evoke Carol's decision to be satisfied with her present lot, to refuse passion; on the other hand, they recall Howard's previous allusion to his sister's composure and contentment. The fifth sentence, from Howard's perspective, allusively refers to previous scenes and thoughts when Carol did not deserve his assent. Faced with these multiple allusions, readers need both intense concentration and associative minds in order to fathom the connections and grasp Carol's defeated ideals.

Further perplexing allusions await the reader. The last section of the story, resuming the action of the first one, begins with an apparently unnecessary allusion to the weather. As Gallant professes that "only the essentials remain" (Girard-Valette, 82) in her stories, the allusion cannot be brushed off as irrelevant. Indeed it refers back to Carol's conviction that once the weather turns better she will fall in love; but it must also connect with future events, the more so as Odile's comment—"This was the longest winter I remember, although I think one says this every year" (21)—alludes to patterns, forgotten and resumed time and again, an allusion that will connect with Carol's approach to marriage: just as seasons come back, her disappointment over her lack of passion will return and will always be followed by her refusal to break the frail bond of her marriage. Of course this realization only comes upon rereading the story; at first, the general implications of the reference to the weather will be lost for want of a wider frame of reference achieved only by retroactive reading.

The analepsis taking the reader back to the first scene of the story allows Odile to mention how she worries about her sister and Felix, and to take Carol along to visit Felix. The walk in that part of town with "crooked, narrow streets," "a section of Paris Carol ha[s] not seen" (22), recalls Carol's conviction that some side street would inspire her love. She does discover love in two ways; first she witnesses Odile and Felix's love (25); second she senses her intimacy with Felix (25) and presents an interesting case of transferral of emotions when Felix lets her know that "Odile loves [her]" (28): "Her heart leaped as if he, Felix, had said he loved her. But no, she corrected herself. Not Felix but some other man, some wonderful person who did not exist" (28). Evidenced by the simile in the first statement, the transferral leaps to another one conveying that Carol reverts to an ideal, not to a reality, repeating a pattern started before. Her dream comes true, but its materialization contrasts her vision of a romantic setting, far from the one she finds herself in:

> For a moment, standing under the noisy trains on the dark, dusty boulevard, she felt that she had at last opened the right door, turned down the right street, glimpsed the vision toward which she had struggled on winter evenings when, standing on the staircase, she had wanted to be enchanted with Paris and to be in love with Howard. (29)

Though the sentence repeats the very words of Carol's original conviction that certain conditions are needed to fall in love (9), the scene ironically contrasts with her vision by presenting a setting alien to her dreams.

At this point the reader wonders what track Carol will choose—love or its appearance? A mental somersault pulls Carol away from her dream as she weighs her emotions and the conditions under which they would flourish, and rejects the whole picture because of its material sordidness; she refuses a vision "com[ing] from Felix and Odile" (29), no matter how much she has longed for it: "she remembered in time what Felix was—a hopeless parasite. And Odile was silly and immoral and old enough to know better. And they were not married and never would be, and they spent heaven knew how many hours in that terrible room in a slummy quarter of Paris" (29). Echoing the discourse of a child, this passage characterized by its abundant coordination reflects how Carol needs to punctuate the negative aspects of Odile and Felix to convince herself to reject the vision. In a similar manner, when she reverts to her relation with Howard, coordinators stress their assets as if she needed to count them: "What she and Howard had was better. No one could point to them, or criticize them, or humiliate them by offering to help" (29). Carol's outlook pushes her away from her ideal into a conventional reality which she will nevertheless romanticize. The conditional used throughout signals a condition likely, though by no means assured:

> Soon, she sensed, the comforting vision of Paris as she had once imagined it would overlap the reality. To have met and married Howard there would sound so romantic and interesting, more and more so as time passed. She would forget the rain and her unshared confusion and loneliness, and remember instead the Paris films, the street lamps with their tinsel icicles, the funny concert hall where the ceiling collapsed, and there would be, at last, a coherent picture, accurate but untrue. The memory of Felix and Odile and their distasteful strangeness would slip away; for "love" she would think, once more, "Paris," and, after a while, happily married, mercifully removed in time, she would remember it and describe it and finally believe it as it never had been at all. (30)

The final paragraph recalls a previous sordid scene made fun of and told with much flourish that causes Carol's awareness about the truthfulness of accounts: "She realized for the first time that something could be perfectly accurate but untruthful—they had not found any part of that evening funny—and that this might cover more areas of experience than the occasional amusing story" (13). Putting the last paragraph in parallel with this sentence, readers eventually visualize the intricate patterns that the story has drawn for them by contrasts and blanks to fill in. Thus the pattern of excitements and the rejection of their source eventually leads to the erasure of any trace of past brief encounters with a disturbing reality, ironically disclosing in-depth disconnection.

The story thus exhibits how Gallant makes the most of ironic contrasts of unsettling perspectives, constantly moving in utterly opposed directions. Now bringing closer, now pulling away, Gallant's writing prevents the reader from even attempting to empathize; any such attempt is indeed frustrated because of the irony or conflicting revelation disclosed every so often. The latter highlight Gallant's understanding of culture from within and without; she conveys their differences by exposing the rather romanticized North American perception of France together with an insider's version revealing some unattractive aspects of French society after the war. With the protagonist's idealized version of Paris contrasting with its real picture, the narrative hints at the human tendency toward self-delusion, the need to stick to an invented vision of life and its concomitant refusal to acknowledge even the existence of another reality. Such need leads to disconnection and instability, the very condition of exile.

Gallant's eye for the ridiculous trait in her characters enhances their unstable position.[6] In "Potter," for instance, she ridicules the self-centredness and lack of perspective of Parisian-based Laurie Bennett, Piotr's Canadian lover: "Her idea of history began with the Vietnam war; Genesis was her own Canadian childhood. [...]He called his beloved 'Lah-ow-rie,' which made her laugh. She could not pronounce 'Piotr' and never tried; she said Peter, Prater, Potter, and Otter, and he answered to all" (*Fifteenth District*, 169). The initial parallel makes the reader smile at Laurie's intellectual limitations and solid ignorance of history. Her "confident unawareness [...] of a contrasting appearance and reality" (Muecke, *Irony*, 35) stresses her lack of connection with the world at large and her inability to relate to others. Taken together, the next two sentences make fun of her narrow-mindedness. On the one hand, her reaction to Piotr's mispronouncing her name shows her inability to understand that others might have differing cultural standards. On the other, she does not seem to fathom her own incompetence, since her problematic pronunciation of Piotr's name is presented from the point of view of a detached, scornful observer, alluding to Piotr's generous acceptance of all the misnomers.

In the face of this "ironic situation" (Muecke, 37), the reader feels both amused and superior, for Piotr's acceptance implies an imposed change of identity. With their ironic symbolic meaning, of which Laurie is certainly unaware, the misnomers further disconnect Piotr from his own sense of self. By calling him Potter, Laurie alludes to the master of matter, to whose hands she pretends to entrust her life (de Vries, 373). Funnily enough, the name suits him perfectly, as, towards the end of the story, he realizes that his love for Laurie was only his creation, that he had created an image of Laurie with which he had fallen in love, proof of Piotr's ill-grounded feelings. As she too eventually understands that she cannot live without him, the name suits Piotr doubly. However, since his creation is merely wishful thinking, the misnomer only increases the sense of futility behind his feelings.

The same holds true for his animal nickname, Otter. Once caught, the North American trickster "pleads not to be thrown into the water and drowned and then, being thrown in, swims away laughing" (Cooper, 171). Emotionally destitute when he understands that Laurie is unfaithful to him, Piotr decides to write about their story, producing a "long wail, [...] a babbling complaint" (201) that encourages his suffering from "bachelor's ailment" (198). Nevertheless, like the otter "who swims away laughing," he eventually sees the true nature of their relationship, which, in spite of his initial rejection of it, helps him keep aloof and contemplate his departure, launching him into another uncertain situation, back to his homeland where he no longer fits.

The change from Piotr to Peter involves no semantic alteration, but shifts the identity from Polish to English. Like many monolinguals who have a liking for such shifts, Laurie is unaware of the personality split they bring about. The change gives a previous passage further significance: "he had long considered himself to be bankrupt—of belief, of love, of licence to choose. Here in Paris he was shackled, held, tied to a visa, then to the system of mysterious favors on which his Polish passport depended" (169). The passage reveals how, on account of his Polish identity, Piotr depends on others, how much he lacks emotional and physical independence. But since he acquires an anglicized first name, he eventually changes and learns from Laurie the ability to "[spend] a legacy of careless freedom with [...] abandon" (169). This allows him, towards the end of the story, to see their relationship in its true perspective. He somehow betrays her trust in the image she has of him, calling to mind his homonym, the leader of the Apostles whose denial of ties with Jesus evidences lack of determination and allegiance, an outsider among outsiders.

As to the last nickname, Prater, it reveals more about Laurie than about Piotr. The one who forever talks excessively or pointlessly is Laurie, not Piotr. A poet and a university lecturer, Piotr nevertheless occasionally makes statements detrimental to his interests, when interrogated by the Polish police about his translation of a mad German poet (183) or when responding to social chitchat at a dinner party in Paris (191). As he misunderstands the rules of the game, he cannot anticipate the consequence of his words and becomes a prater rather than an intelligent conversationalist, relegating himself to a corner.

In a comment on Laurie, the narrator highlights how unfair she can be, stating as its cause the very source of irony: "If she took some forms of injustice for granted, it was because she did not know they were unjust" (169–70). Typical of irony, her unawareness leads to hilarious situations: "Piotr was supposed to know by *instinct* every shade of difference between Victoria, British Columbia, and Charlottetown, Prince Edward Island, whereas he, poor Potter, came out of a cloudy Eastern plain bereft of roads, schools, buses, elevators, perhaps even frontiers—this because she could not have found Warsaw on a map" (170). Not only is her assumption laughable, for it implies knowledge prior to any actual experience, but her own incapacity to stand the test is mocked, the more so as the image she has of Poland reminds one of the North American ignoramus who thinks that all places unknown to him/her are necessarily the dwelling places of savages. Her lack of basic intelligence, recorded in her incompetent reading of maps, is, of course, ridiculed and her position as an unilluminated outsider strengthened.

Gallant's mockery does not stop there. She goes on describing Laurie's conversational achievements, highlighting her basic ignorance. When she first meets Piotr, she tells him, "If Solzhenitsyn were to walk in here, I'd get right down on my knees and thank him" (173). Surprised, Piotr asks her "What for?" "I don't know," she answers. "I thought you might. [...] I was just trying to show you I sympathized" (173). Having no sense of ridicule, she makes such nonsensical comments "to please; it [is] [her] way of paying a compliment to someone she consider[s] clever" (176). Time and again, she exposes her ignorance, accounted for by her lack of "memory, except of her schooldays" (175). Caustically, the narrator compares her to "a blackboard wiped clean every week or so" (175). To no one's surprise, Laurie's ignorance is matched by her stupidity:

> It seemed incredible that a man of his education knew nothing about Bishop Purse School or its famous headmistress, Miss Ellen Jones. Bishop, whatever its advantages, had not darkened Laurie's sunny intelligence with anything like geography, history, or simple arithmetic. She had the handwriting of a small boy and could not spell her own language. For a time Piotr treasured a letter in which

> he was described as 'a really sensative [sic] person,' and Laurie herself as 'mixed-up in some ways but on the whole pretty chearfull [sic]'. (170)

The combined voices which describe Laurie contribute to the derisive quality of the passage. At first, Laurie's voice is heard within the discourse of the narrator, effecting a clash of views: Laurie's incredulity at Piotr's ignorance is pitted against the narrator's enlightened recognition of its normality. The next two sentences render facts dispassionately, silencing Laurie's voice and exposing both Laurie and Piotr to ridicule. Her stupidity and lack of basic knowledge conveyed obliquely match her childlike handwriting and atrocious spelling; as she is made fun of, so is Piotr because, though well educated, he paradoxically cherishes her the more for her intellectual shortcomings, as if they guaranteed her innocence.

If Gallant subjects Laurie to stinging ridicule, she turns to Piotr with gentle irony.[7] Though she makes fun of his weaknesses, she does not sneeringly pierce her description of him. She rather conveys her understanding of the deprivation ruining his life through forgiving irony. She makes the reader grasp why Piotr loves such a shallow being as Laurie; the product of her education, her typical carelessness seduces him beyond comprehension because it opens up new horizons, making him feel some forthcoming connection. In sharp contrast to the binding and alienating realities inherent in the Communist system, Laurie's neutral and privileged Canadian experience turns her into an easygoing being making no demands on Piotr, who in turn cherishes her unconditionally. Blinded with infatuation, Piotr does not decode Laurie's messages properly and fails to realize that all the postcards she sends him to Poland are written on trips she makes with another man. Finally managing to get back to Paris, he enjoys a blissful, though short-lived reunion; on account of his sudden discovery of her impending trip to Venice with an unnamed friend, his passion turns into grief and jealousy strong enough to disconnect him from his own self: "His work, his childhood, his imprisonment, his marriage, his still mysterious death were rolled in a compact ball, spinning along the grass, away from whatever was left of him" (186). His newly acquired knowledge makes him see, like Gallant, "the element of farce in every iniquity" (186), for he realizes his gift of Polish contraceptives was foolish. He suffers from all sorts of ailments—psychosomatic manifestations of his distress and disjunction, as ironically pointed out by a pushy admirer of his—until the relationship is restored with Laurie's pitiful comeback. But Piotr has to leave the country prematurely the day after Laurie returns to him, situational irony being at hand. His departure results from his French exchange professor's expulsion from Poland after "finding her students materialistic and coarsely bourgeois [...] [and trying] to fire them with revolutionary ideals" (205). This farcical reversal of expectations is matched by another, Piotr's invention that after all he only feels tenderness for Laurie, an invention prompted by Laurie's need to be loved, which would trap him. The final sentences of the story pit his voice against the omniscient narrator's, creating a comic alternation of the truthful and the invented version behind Piotr's refusal to respond to Laurie's need: "An immense weight of blame crushed him, flattened him, and by so doing cleansed and absolved him. I was incapable of any more feeling than this. I never felt more than kindness. There was nothing in it from the beginning. It was only tenderness after all" (212). Connection cannot be reached in the exiles' lives.

Gallant pokes fun at other characters in "Potter" while emphasizing their marginality. Marek, Piotr's Polish émigré friend with strategic connections, has such a marginal position in Parisian society that each time he opens doors for Piotr he fears that the latter might blunder, thereby enforcing exclusion for both from circles not usually open to foreigners. Prior to the exclusive dinner party given by a famous French hostess, Marek briefs Piotr with a comic sense of urgency: "Piotr was not to contradict anything, even if he knew it to be inaccurate; above all, he was not to imagine that anything said to him was ever meant to be funny" (190). The content of the advice, of course, leaves no doubt as to the underlying sarcastic intention. Both Marek and the French elite are smiled at, the one for his desperate clinging to the other's favours that help him climb the social ladder, the other for not accepting other people's conflicting views. Similarly, Gallant offers an amusing picture of the doctor with whom Piotr stays; unhappily married to a man who spends his Sundays with his mistress and illegitimate daughter, the doctor hints at her loneliness, hoping to evoke a similar response from Piotr and to establish good grounds for a love affair. Hers is the predatory approach of the emotional exile, and Gallant holds it in derision.

In "His Mother," Gallant directs her irony at the mother of an émigré and the circle of émigrés' mothers to which she belongs. Her attitude, even before her son's departure, is laughed at explicitly for it exposes her lack of grounding; Gallant obviously makes fun of the hidden discourse underlying most parent/child conversation by opposing the said and the unsaid:

> He was a stone out of a stony generation. Talking to him was like lifting a stone out of water. He never resisted, but if you let go for even a second he sank and came to rest on a dark sea floor [...] How could she give up? She loved him. She felt shamed because it had not been in her to control armies, history, his stony watery world. From the moment he appeared in the kitchen doorway, passive, vacant, starting to live again only because this was morning, she began all over: "Don't you feel well?" "Are you all right?" "Why can't you smile?"—though the loudest sentence was in silence: Ask me how I am." (214)

Built around the two middle, particularly short, sentences that are like a cry of love, the longer sentences contextually stress the doubtful truthfulness of the mother's feelings, particularly because of the initial metaphor and its elaboration. Their insincerity is confirmed by the final chopped up sentence with the string of questions that explicitly conceal one statement, begging for attention; the shorter section of the final balanced sentence after the questions supposed to mark genuine interest forcefully points to the woman's self-centeredness and inability to relate to her son.

Further contextual indices mark Gallant's ironic intentions:

> After he left Budapest (got his first passport, flew to Glasgow with a soccer team, never came back) she became another sort of a person, an émigré's mother. She shed the last of her unimportant lovers and with the money her son was soon able to send she bought a white blouse, combs that would pin her hair away from her face, and a blue kimono. She remembered long, tender conversations they had had together, and she got up early in the morning to see if a letter had come from him and then to write one of her own describing everything she thought and did. (214)

The short triadic sentence in parenthesis marks a series of facts seen as the cause for her to change costumes and take a different part in the societal play—that of an émigré's mother—with falsified memories attached.[8] The status thus acquired in itself justifies the drastic change from slovenly to dignified appearance, from attached to proudly single, that might have agreed with the son before his departure.

Gallant goes on describing the hilarious ranking system among the émigrés' mothers: "The aristocrats were those whose children had never left Europe; the poorest of the poor were not likely ever to see their sons again, for they had gone to Chile and South Africa. Switzerland was superior to California. A city earned more points than a town. There was no mistaking her precedence here; she was a duchess" (215). Entertaining, the whole system of appraisal reduces emotions to nought. The same happens with letters and presents; according to their nature, they confer on the receiver credentials of varying importance. A mother of a silent émigré, therefore, enjoys no status whatsoever; her son "might as well be dead" (216). Paradoxically, in spite of her credentials, the title character realizes she is not better off; although she does not think of her son as dead, a corrective statement—"but as a coin that had dropped unheard, had rolled crazily, lay still" (216)—implies that for all intents and purposes "he might as well be dead."

Her own letters with descriptions of her dreams or of the town manifest the distance that separates her from her son. Her dreams of resurrecting dead people echo the reality of her life. For though alive, her son is caught "between the dead and the living, a voice on the telephone, an affectionate letter full of English words, a coin rolled and lying somewhere in secret" (223); her sadness, if not bitterness, makes her accumulate metaphors reflecting the absence of her son, indeed his inanimate presence. Cynical, she knows she is only "the revered and respected mother of a generous, an attentive, a camouflaged stranger" (223); initial and final qualifiers evidence an unwanted reality—she is an image, a mother on paper, not in actual fact. The descriptions of the town finish with a description of the émigrés' mothers' haunt and an anguished question asked as if the son would come to visit—"will you know me? I was your mother" (224). Contrasting the future and the past, the question and statement thereafter obliquely express her present anguished need of recognition and aimlessness owing to her lost role in her son's life. An emotional pauper, she stands on the shaky grounds of outsiders.

"The Other Paris," "Potter," and "His Mother" do not stand out as an exception in Gallant's oeuvre. All her short stories and novellas present in semi-serious tone the aberrations of the system in which, or by which, her characters live, turning them all into exiles of sorts. Even stories that are heavily autobiographical, like the Linnet Muir sequence, for instance, have ironic undertones revealing her awareness of the discrepancy between the real and the ideal, pointing to "the contrast of 'appearance' and 'reality' " (Muecke, *Irony and Ironic*, 44). The analysis of "The Other Paris" has emphasized the characters' need to idealize reality and revealed the discrepancy between the views of one set of characters and another. In other stories with split levels of narration, such as "The Pegnitz Junction" and "The Old Friends," the ironic use of intertextual and contextual references powerfully points out how people cannot relate to others truthfully. In the stories rewriting history, human indifference, segregation, and disconnectedness emerge from the derisive treatment of the characters and their actions as well as from the constant references to history and its representation. As Blodgett notes, "it is as though the unfolding of her text were a game of I Ching played with both the self and history, each design projecting a certain significance only to be immediately modified by the next, everything in order and everything changing simultaneously at random" (3). The narratives are given an ironic twist by the hints to previous realities that the characters, consciously or unconsciously, erase from their memory, in their search for a truth setting their mind at rest [9]. Gallant accommodates the present by reinscribing the past in such a way as to satisfy the needs of the characters; since the latter cannot cope with the traditional versions of the past, they are shown reinventing it. Contextuality adds a corrective subtext, no doubt ironic in impact, as it reveals the fundamentally subjective perception of the past, virtually made up from start to finish, to assuage the characters' feelings of guilt. The same holds for characters trying to erase the unpleasant reality of their lives, pretending to be grounded when they actually fail to establish firm bonds with anyone, let alone with themselves.

Such a depressing certainty can only be counteracted by a measure of irony that combines contradictory concepts. Gallant does this so adroitly that "people sometimes take seriously things [she means] as a joke" (Hancock 52). I would argue that this essentially results from the dispassionate grounding of her stories in culture. Take her Canadian, French and German stories, or her stories about British exiles on the Riviera in *From the Fifteenth District*, to mention but a few—they all bear on the essence of the characters' culture. Only the open-minded insider can decipher the double layers of meaning; the obtuse insider or the outsider is likely to take every word at its face value and miss the irony which "[engages] its critique from the inside of that which it contests" (Hutcheon, "Introduction," 13). Gallant indeed describes a world she knows well, a world of which she has first-hand experience or on which she has a multiple perspective. Her penetrating gaze fixes the ways in which people function within a system that is originally theirs (as in the stories featuring Canadians at home, and in the German and Parisian stories) or inherited by choice (as in the stories featuring Canadians and Americans abroad, exiles on the Riviera, expatriates in Paris). Never does she openly take sides; rather, she remains aloof, evaluating the extent of human aberration. Thus she describes from a detached perspective, supposedly neutrally, characteristics that turn out to be rather ludicrous; hers is "a complex narrative mode involving both implication in the story and critical distance from it" (LaCapra, 174), the true ironic eye catching the inconsistencies of the characters.

Endowed with the gift of irony, Gallant achieves a special effect when she makes fun, either teasingly or piercingly, of her characters, their views and situations. An expert in the art of polyphony, Gallant uses this device to pit one voice against another and also to undermine a situation while distancing herself from it. In this way, she can easily portray breaks of continuity in history, thereby creating tension: in her work, neither continuity nor stability exist, and one perspective never predominates—all her characters are exiles in one way or another. Her irony thus "deconstructs one discourse [...] as it constructs another" (Hutcheon, "Introduction," 16), offering the possibility of putting two levels of meaning together, and as a consequence, causing split levels of discourse, the very reflection of the split characterizing exiles. Gallant's stories could be compared to a picture and its negative. Shown both at once, readers see that what is white on the one is black on the other, and vice versa. Owing to the superimposition, they perceive both the positive and the negative aspects of anything, sensing the ironic fusion of opposites. Such a perspective is destabilizing; it offers no security. Everyone is constantly exposed to the ironic pen offering at once a usually harmless surface reading and a deeper, often critical, reading. Grounded in two levels, the text never allows readers to gain a firm footing; certainties are forever beyond their grasp, just as they are for the characters. In this respect, Gallant's outlook is definitely postmodern, for as Hutcheon argues "postmodern irony is suspicious of any [...] claim to transcendence, universality and power" (Hutcheon, "Power," 35); it never accepts facile resolutions, never takes things at their face value—in short it never fails to take in the contradictions, the uncertainties and marginality of any being.

In Gallant's eyes, irony flickers; in her heart, she hides the need to subvert human fate. Playing on the explicit and the implicit, Gallant has a "way of writing designed to leave open the question of what literal meaning might signify"; her irony deconstructs and constructs while "[activating] not one but an endless series of subversive interpretations" (Muecke, *Irony and Ironic*, 31). In the first place, her ironic touch "works to distance, undermine, unmask, relativize, destabilize" (Hutcheon, "Introduction," 30); secondly, she opens up different readings of her fiction and the world, whereby she enables the reader to confront history with its contra/dictions; thirdly she grasps the disconnectedness of the exile. Finally, in order to convey the overall sense of disconnectedness prevailing in Gallant's characters' experience, I'd like to offer a sub/version of her titles, an ironic "intervention" of her writing. "Overhead in a balloon" rather than hopping "from cloud to cloud," the author sees through the characters' loss of self, their vanished "image on the mirror." Caught "in plain sight," "in the tunnel" "between zero and one," the characters are trapped in countless "varieties of exile," their "voices lost in snow." Exiles of the self, forever "in transit," they look for "the other Paris" as they drift "across the bridge," unless they are marooned at "the Pegnitz Junction" or at "the end of the world." As no one can "let it pass," the "state of affairs" can only be like "an emergency case" after an "accident." Aimlessly wandering in "the circus" of their deconstructing attempts to build themselves a nest behind "three brick walls," they are hoping for "better times" that will never come; there will be no "remission," only "a painful affair." Like an "April fish" deceptively promising "a flying start," any consideration of serious "questions and answers" is bound to end up in "careless talk." Therefore "the old friends" can never find a "lasting peace," the one always being the "alien flower" of the other, fearing "rejection." Since their "heart[s are] broken," because "acceptance of their ways" never emanates from anyone, the characters and the readers alike face the same reality: Gallant's short fiction hammers out the message that there is no Truth "with a capital T." Fragmented worlds, such are the "home truths" of Mavis Gallant's short fiction.

Postmod Irony — suspicious of any claim to transcendence [illegible]

① Irony — never accepts
- facile resolutions
- face value
takes in contradictions uncertainties

to distance
" undermine
" unmask
" relativize
" destabilize

Overall sense of disconnectedness

Notes

1. See Godard (72–99) for an enlightening discussion of irony in *A Fairly Good Time*, "Good Morning and Goodbye," "Three Brick Walls," "The Flowers of Spring," and "The Other Paris."
2. Besner devotes a whole article to the four opening paragraphs of "The Moslem Wife," showing how important irony is in Gallant's work.
3. See Siemerling (131–53) for a discussion of irony in "Grippes and Poche," "The Other Paris," "About Geneva," and *Green Water, Green Sky*.
4. A story favoured by many, "The Other Paris" has been the subject of numerous critiques, amongst others by Besner (*Light*, 10–17), Keefer (*Reading*, 139–141), and Hatch (94–7). The special Gallant issue of *Essays on Canadian Writing* (42, 1990) includes articles dealing with the story (see Godard, 89–95; and Siemerling, 138–143).
5. For a detailed analysis of memory's ghosts, see Besner (*Light*, 27–38). Fo a discussion of the narrator's questionable authority, see Jewison (100–2).
6. For a detailed analysis of "Potter," see Besner (*Light*, 94–99).
7. Gallant exhibits gentle irony toward characters for whom she feels compassion, such as Carmela in "The Four Seasons," or Molly, James, and Will in "The Remission."
8. The omission of coordinators in the elliptical triadic sentence renders the forcefulness of his escapade palpable, justifying the drastic change in her, a sort of poetic mirroring.
9. Borges' story "Tlön, Uqbar, Orbis Tertius" clarifies such a modification of the past by mentioning that "in all memories, a fictitious part occupies the place of any other. We know nothing about it with any certainty, not even that it is false" (33). This helps to explain the similar perception of life that has allowed archaeologists "to question and even modify the past, which nowadays is no less malleable or obedient than the future" (29).

“Radiant Paradigms and Chinks of Light”

Mavis Gallant’s Polish Émigrés in Paris

Janice Kulyk Keefer

“If we are moved by a story, it has meant something, perhaps something important to us; if we are not moved, then it is, as story, meaningless” (Geddes, 817). I’ve adapted this remark of T.S. Eliot to remind us that whatever our theoretical orientation or critical practice, we must be passionate readers—resistant, yes, but also responsive to what complex literary texts have to offer us, attentive to the terms they work within. It behooves us, in other words, to be moved by what we read, and what we choose to write upon.

“Forain” and “A State of Affairs,” two of Mavis Gallant’s more recent stories, seem to me to be among the most moving works in her oeuvre—moving precisely because of the obliquity with which she approaches the inherently elegiac nature of her subject: the last remnants of the Polish émigré community in Paris—those émigrés who arrived, that is, in the decade following the end of World War II. Perhaps I find these texts particularly moving because of my own “Polish connection,” or perhaps it is because of the tenderness with which Gallant describes the love between husband and wife in both stories, and the attention she pays to what Irving Layton, in his elegy for Keine Lazarovitch, has called “the inescapable lousiness of growing old” (Geddes, 210). At any rate, I hope to offer you a reading of “Forain” and “A State of Affairs” that will illuminate how these stories mean and how they move us.

The fictive worlds Gallant creates in these texts are structurally complex, ironically charged, historically engaged, and the prose through which those worlds unfold is, as always, beautifully intelligent. “Forain” and “A State of Affairs” are in some ways mirror images of each other, with the important difference that the former is told from the point of view of Blaise Forain, a dubious Parisian publisher of Eastern European literature in translation, while the latter is given us from the perspective of Mr Wroblewski, an elderly Polish émigré, whose occasionally mistaken perceptions, not always reliable memories, and fictionalizing desires make him in some ways as problematic a focalizer as Blaise Forain.

"Forain" opens on a leaden winter day, with the funeral of Adam Tremski, a Polish Jew who has perished of "mortal grief" (*Selected Stories*, 637) at the death, not long before his own, of his wife Barbara. Mr Wroblewski, of "A State of Affairs"—the phrase is his euphemism for words like ''problem,'' ''difficulty,'' ''catastrophe'' (648)—is in precarious health and his wife Magda is afflicted by Alzheimer's, though the disease is never named as such. Both Tremski and Wroblewski are historically marked men: Wroblewski, though not Jewish, survived internment at Dachau—what Tremski went though during the war is alluded to by a charcoal portrait of him done in June 1945: "a face that had come through: only just" (638). Barbara, who left her Polish officer husband for life with the seedy, entropic Tremski, rescuing him from his hopeless incapacity for business, and Magda, a former musician and teacher, are women of exemplary intelligence and beauty: stunning in their youth, they retain their attractiveness and elegance in old age. Their husbands deserve them, *tout court*: they possess an integrity and selflessness that make them two of the most sympathetic men in Gallant's oeuvre. When Tremski falls apart after Barbara's death, becoming incapable of shaving or putting his false teeth in; when Mr Wroblewski lies to a friend in Warsaw about the conversation on Schubert he's just held with the minimally capable Magda, it breaks your heart. The marriages between Adam and Barbara, Maciek and Magda are defined by mutual love, loyalty, and respect—qualities rare enough to find between the numerous husbands and wives depicted in Gallant's fiction.

"All that is personal soon rots; it must be packed in ice or salt," or so Yeats advises us (*Selected Poetry*, xx). Masterful touches of ice and salt are provided in "Forain and "A State of Affairs" in ways which bring to mind Nabokov's use of irony and satire to camouflage the outright tenderness with which, for example, he represents Krug's wife and child in *Bend Sinister*, or his own wife and child in *Speak Memory*. In her exposure of the unscrupulousness of a publisher more concerned with the profit than with the poetic motive, and her introduction, into the lives of the Wroblewskis, of a bank official who first offers and then withdraws a vital service which would have eased Mr Wroblewski's mind regarding his invalid wife, Gallant deflects our attention from the pathos of the émigrés to the complexities and ironies of the contexts—social, cultural, historical—in which that pathos achieves such memorable expression.

Elegy, in other words, goes hand in hand with exposure, with the utterly deft critique of social forms and values that has always distinguished not only Gallant's fiction, but also her early journalism, and the essays and narratives collected in *Paris Notebooks*. Thus in "Forain," our glimpse of the generation of old, post-war Polish émigrés, in mourning not only for lost friends "but for all the broken ties and old, unwilling journeys" (627) is supplemented by a succinct, caustic view of the new, post-Wall generation of mobile or migrant Poles who come to Paris not to escape persecution, but to lead more exciting, and more materially rewarding lives. The "thin, pretty girl, part of the recent, non-political emigration" who comes to work for Forain's company has no compunctions about faking the last chapter of Tremski's unfinished manuscript, or about "spreading the story that Forain had been the lover of Barbara" (641). However wittily presented, these falsifications of Tremski's manuscript and of Barbara's memory bring to mind that signal act of desecration referred to in "A State of Affairs''— Sartre's urinating on Chateaubriand's grave at St-Malo.

The "filth that can wash over quiet lives," the "violations" of ordinary human decency (650) are linked by Gallant not only to Sartre's clownish gesture, and, more chillingly, to the anti-semitism which still erupts in Warsaw, but also to the surveillance and harassment of immigrants in contemporary Paris, immigrants without the cachet of the Polish émigrés, with their Nansen passports. In "Forain," Gallant gives us a glimpse of "lines of immigrants standing along the north side of central police headquarters" with "Algerians in a separate queue" (638). She singles out the Portuguese taxi driver intimidated by Forain at the end of the story, and the waiter who cheats Forain of his wine at a café—a young, clumsy man with "coarse fair hair: foreign, probably working without papers, in the shadow of the most powerful police in France" (638). The xenophobia of the French, the plight of the involuntarily "displaced and dispossessed"

(629) to which Gallant has drawn our attention for the past forty years or more—that these issues find a place in "Forain" bears witness to the inclusiveness of Gallant's vision, the rigorous nature of her sympathy, which refuses to restrict itself to whatever is in moral fashion. In "A State of Affairs," we are reminded that "In Paris [...] the entire life of every immigrant is lodged inside a computer or crammed between the cardboard covers of a dossier held together with frayed cotton tape" (647). This kind of scrutiny is presumably an advance upon conditions "in the old days," when refusal of applications for French citizenship by people like the Wroblewskis "was so consistent that one was discouraged at the outset" from applying (649). Though Marie-Louise, sent by the city's social services to help care for the helpless Magda, has automatic French citizenship due to her birth in Martinique, what Gallant emphasizes as a donnée of contemporary Parisian life is the radical insecurity that afflicts the lives of migrants, whether from Poland or Algeria. As Gallant presents it in "Forain" and "A State of Affairs," Paris is a city of highly selective light, of corporate castles and child beggars.

***

Among the new wave of arrivals from Lech Walesa's Poland, "Forain" shows us, are scholars seeking out their displaced compatriots in order to chronicle and evaluate what has ceased to be lived experience and become "history": "Scholars who looked dismayingly youthful, speaking the same language, but with a new, jarring vocabulary [...] taping reminiscences, copying old letters" (628). Yet their subjects, instead of feeling gratitude at this validation of their lives, are not impressed: "History turned out to be a plodding science. What most émigrés settled for now was the haphazard accuracy of a memory like Tremski's" (629).

Adam Tremski, of course, is Gallant's invention. He is the most distinguished of Forain's "flock" (634) of East and Central European émigré writers—unlike the others, he could have found a better publisher, just as he could have moved up from the shabby, standard-issue émigré apartment he still occupied at his death. Nevertheless he does not join "the leviathan prophets, the booming novelists, the great mentors and tireless definers" lionized in the West (634), but remains in the company of those "self-effacing, flat-broke writers who [had] asked only to be read, believing they had something to say that was crucial to the West, that might even goad it into action" (637). Gallant doesn't spare these ingenuous, unworldly writers any irony: we learn that even the intelligent Tremski believed that a "great new war would leave central Europe untouched. The liberating missiles would sail across without ruffling the topmost leaf of a poplar tree." Ingenuousness, however, is matched by a wry embrace of sauve-qui-peut: "As for the contenders, well, perhaps their time was up" (637).

Gallant is especially perceptive about the plight of those writers, who, much to Blaise Forain's chagrin, continue long past 1989 to write "stories in which Socialist incoherence was matched by Western irrelevance" (636). Though these accounts of the "East-West dilemma" may be of historical value, their critique of 'the Way of the West' still valid, they are unmarketable, and thus unpublishable. Besides, even in the heyday of the Cold War, most Western readers had not been able to keep straight the names of Forain's various writers, and reviewers had rarely mentioned their work. Now the barbarism of the French reading public (635) is aggravated by the no less barbaric dictates of the Market Economy, for which money and memory have become interdependent. When the Berlin Wall came down, we learn, it brought with it the fortunes, such as they were, of Blaise Editions, causing an irreversible and catastrophic decline in sales. Whereas the Wall can be "hammered to still smaller pieces and sold all over the world," the work of Forain's authors can't. The satiric edge of Gallant's humour makes the situation more rather than less emphatic, as analogies are drawn between the (presumed) End of Communism and Vatican II's axeing of the traditional Mass, so that publishers of prayer books in Latin and of "subtle and allusive stud[ies] of corruption in Minsk," circa 1973 (636), stand side by side in bankruptcy court. As for the members of Forain's flock, they would seem destined for the fate of double disappearance, their manuscripts rotting unread as they themselves die off.

Blaise Forain is one of the more hapless and engaging of Gallant's rogues: initially, at least, it is his honesty that quiets our unease at the way he operates. If he is "unreliable" (634) about paying his flock of writers their dues, it is not to get rich at their expense. He has "next to no money," we are told, and is "in continual debt to printers and banks" (634); quite sensibly, he needs to turn a profit—equally sensibly, he would prefer to be given the cash spent by Central and European embassies on gold medals and lavish receptions to mark the cultural service he has rendered to the "other Europe." If it is a question of medals or money, there is no question— despite the fiction in government circles that "trade and literature are supposed to have no connection" (635). But at certain points after Tremski's death, we are made aware of how the publisher is compromising his already-fraught integrity. Not only does Forain toy with the idea of effectively cannibalizing the lives and work of his "flock" to produce a "sly, quiet novel teasingly based on" [Chekhov's *The Cherry Orchard*] and set in the new, unified Germany (636), but a year after Tremski's death, Forain persuades himself that the man who'd made him his literary executor would have approved of the last chapter of an unfinished manuscript being "knitted up from fragments he had left trailing" (641). But even worse than Forain's publishing of Tremski's adulterated manuscript is his shift of allegiance from the Tremskis to the writer's stepdaughter, the crassly resentful, unintelligent Halina. When he catches himself in this act of disloyalty, Forain promises himself, head bowed as if in prayer, that "he would keep in mind things as they once were, not as they seemed to him now" (641)—a crucial task, one would think, for someone who "wanted every work he published to survive in collective memory, even when the paper it was printed on had been pulped, burned in the city's vast incinerators or lay moldering at the bottom of the Seine" (635). Forain's pious gesture at the end of this story, however, only leads him to "make a fool of himself to no purpose" (641), becoming a confrère of Halina's father who had fought a "war for nothing" (632).

***

The problematic role played in "Forain" by the preserver, disseminator, and adulterator of Tremski's work is transformed in "A State of Affairs" to the less complex intervention of a Fournier, rather than a Forain—the bank employee who summons Mr Wroblewski to her office to present him with a gift far more useful than the Christmas chocolates distributed to the elderly every year by the Mayor of Paris. This gift is a cash reserve from which he can draw, at times of need, without paying interest. The soul of courtesy, Mr Wroblewski undergoes an interview with Carole Fournier, explaining how important this cash reserve will be for his wife, should he predecease her. But when Mme Fournier learns Mr Wroblewski's age, and calculates the cost to him of undergoing the medical examinations the bank would demand of him, she withdraws the offer. Perhaps the émigré's only gain from the interview is a memory triggered by the sight of Carole Fournier's profile —the memory of Elzbieta Barszczewska, a wildly popular Polish actress of the interwar years. This incident seems trivial compared to the fact exposed at the end of the interview—that Mr Wroblewski's greatest problem is his own inevitable and impending death (654). And yet, on the story's final page, it is to Barszczewska that Wroblewski alludes in the poignantly deceptive letter he composes to his friend in Warsaw, summoning the shared memories of their youth.

Carole Fournier is, of course, a far less important and malign presence than Blaise Forain, but her embarrassment and panic at Mr Wroblewski's allusion to the fact of mortality have a particular significance. For Fournier is the product of an age in which azure computer screens, not God, "sugges[t] the infinite" (651), and where the mirror-glass of office towers masquerade as the sky. The information age, and the age of market values, Gallant seems to suggest, are anathema to both the preservation of memory and the consciousness of history: the antithesis to the computer screen in Fournier's office is, of course, the exchange of letters between Mr Wroblewski and his friend in Warsaw—the "dead" letters, too, which Magda writes, letters which, we are told, would be perfectly apropos if they'd been written forty-five years ago.

Mr Wroblewski's persistent connection to his unnamed correspondent in Warsaw—the thought of whom, he confesses, never quits him (654), is the trace, in this story, of that "angel of history" which haunts so much of Gallant's fiction—memory not as nostalgia, or passive reflection of the past, but as the painfully active desire to "stay in place, resurrect the dead and reconstruct the wreckage" (Lichtheim,12). The memory of Mr Wroblewski's Warsaw friend is "completely alert" (643), so that the hate mail and death threat he receives after speaking in a radio broadcast of his experiences in the Warsaw ghetto reconfirm his earlier experiences of Polish anti-semitism as something bred in "the brain, blood and bone" (642). Mr Wroblewski's own memory—and conscience—is alert enough to catch, in his friend's disclaimer—"I don't mean this for you. You were always different" (642) —a distressing echo of what Wroblewski himself may have said to this same friend some fifty years ago, when the vilification of Jews was rampant in Poland: "Naturally you are completely different: I'm talking about all the others" (643).

That an elderly man should be sent a death threat for recalling to public memory horrific events and the shameful prejudices which contributed to those events is "the dark riddle" (63) woven into "A State of Affairs," one which grimly counterpoints the donnée of the story—an elderly man's impending death "in a foreign city" (631). And it is no accident that the collective amnesia which has seized hold of post-Wall Europe—if not entrenched long before—is foregrounded in "Forain." Barbara's daughter from her first marriage is unable or unwilling to convey the importance of Tremski's work to her French husband, or to their twelve-year-old daughter. Unlike Magda Wroblewski, whom memory has abandoned except in cruelly selective ways, Halina chooses not to know, and not to remember. She is not alone, of course, as we learn from one of the story's more devastating aperçus:

> It was remarkable, Tremski had said, the way literate people, reasonably well travelled and educated, comfortably off, could live adequate lives without wanting to know what had gone before or happened elsewhere. (630)

Among the literate are journalists who substitute "a few names, a date looked up, a notion of geography" (631) for a sustained form of historical consciousness.

Any such consciousness is, of course, dependent on memory, which, as Gallant's oeuvre has so convincingly shown, is notoriously capricious or unreliable, and yet which remains crucial to the preservation of human decency and dignity. Memory is dependent, in "Forain" and "A State of Affairs," on the material as well as the imagined: the Nansen passports Mr Wroblewski is so apprehensive about surrendering to the State, the 1950s apartment Tremski refuses to quit: "two rooms on a court, windowless kitchen, splintered floors, unheatable bathroom, no elevator, intimidating landlord" (628). Tremski's attachment to the physical traces of the past is his way of keeping faith with memory. It seems entirely fitting that Forain's prayer for the repose of Tremski's soul comes in the form of a mental inventory of the contents of the writer's apartment. There is something unbearably poignant about this list of objects soon to vanish—layers of coats on pegs, boots and umbrellas, unread newspapers and journals, shelves of books and empty or overflowing files, and photographs of friends from the 50s and 60s. The unopened crates and boxes littering the place remind us of Tremski's essential homelessness, that he never seemed really to have moved into this apartment where he lived for some forty years (640). The table that serves for both writing and eating, the narrow couch that doubles as Halina's bed, the window providing "the sort of view that prisoners see" (637)—all of these remind me of the dismally cramped apartments one finds in former Soviet bloc countries, and in which all too many people are still compelled to live out their lives.

In "A State of Affairs," the equivalent of, or counter to, Tremski's apartment, is the bust of Magda made by an impoverished émigré sculptor. Because the work was never cast, no trace of the likeness remains, for the original was lost or broken long ago. The absence of this material record of Magda's youth is especially devastating to Mr Wroblewski, since it was through this work of art, we learn, that he first came to understand his wife's beauty (648). But it's not just the loss of the distant past, but the erasure, as well, of the immediate past that Mr Wroblewski finds so distressing—the unexplained cutting down, for example, of a stand of trees in his neighbourhood, an absence which, ironically, the otherwise oblivious Magda points out to him.

In this context, then, the demolition of the Berlin Wall becomes especially significant. Hateful as it was, the wall offered what Forain calls a "radiant paradigm," whereby the world could be divided, with Manichean neatness, into good and evil, truth and lies, the desirable and the abominable. With the disappearance of the Wall, more is lost than Blaise Forain's solvency: the paradigm it offered may have been fictive, but it formed a focus for that moral discourse Auden describes in "September 1, 1939"—those "ironic points of light" that "Flash out wherever the Just/Exchange their messages" (*Selected Poems*, 89)—the kind of discourse Tremski and his fellow émigré writers helped to sustain.

In "A State of Affairs," that "radiant paradigm" has shrunk to mere "chinks of light" (643)—what Mr Wroblewski would like to show his Jewish friend to displace the "dark riddle" of racial hatred. Were this friend able to travel to Paris, Mr Wroblewski believes, he would encounter the "jovial, generous, welcoming" mood of "One Europe, One World" (643), a Europe in which no one will suffer for being thought a stranger, a foreigner, an outsider. In Mr Wroblewski's fantasies, the two elderly men would sit together in a Montparnasse café to discuss "the news and [...] what it means" in a world that can be judged by something as innocuous as the colours reflected by the glassed office buildings: "pale gold, gray, white and blue" (654). It is not difficult to construe what Mr Wroblewski's friend, given his "amazing memory of events," his ability to supply a "historical context for everything" (643), would make of such "chinks of light" as the new Europe affords. The endings of "Forain" and "A State of Affairs" offer ironic parallels between the deceptions and disloyalty practiced by Blaise Forain towards Adam Tremski, and the heartbreaking lies told by Mr Wroblewski to his Warsaw friend about Magda's fine health and his own unruffled state of mind.

***

> "In the end it was always a poem that ran through the mind—not a string of dates" (629).

The poem that runs through "Forain" and "A State of Affairs" is an elegy for the "displaced and dispossessed" (628). I would like to end this paper by looking at the imagery of darkness and light through which this poem comes to haunt Gallant's prose, and to move us towards a perception of our own moral riddles, our own mortality.

Most of the mourners at Adam Tremski's funeral are elderly Polish émigrés, some of whom have "migrated to high-rise apartments in the outer suburbs, to deeper loneliness and cheaper rents" (630).

> Some had spent all these years in France without social security or health insurance, either for want of means or because they had never found their feet in the right sort of employment. Possibly they believed that a long life was in itself full payment for a safe old age. Should the end turn out to be costly and prolonged, then, please, allow us to dream and float in the thickest, deepest darkness, unaware of the inconvenience and clerical work we may cause. (632-3)

That "thickest, deepest darkness"—a dearly-earned oblivion—makes the "glitter and well-being" (640) of material prosperity in Paris more than a little suspect: though "Every light in the city [may be] ablaze in the dark rain" (640), we can infer that to most émigrés these "lighted windows see[m] exclusive, like careless snubs" (651). In "A State of Affairs", we learn how the Wroblewskis have put behind them the "gray dawns" of emigrant neediness, the begging—but not the crawling—for "enough to eat, relief from pain, a passport, employment" (646). Yet between the azure computer screen of Carole Fournier and the mirror facade of the Montparnasse tower, "a sheet of black glass [that] means nothing" (654), what is there for them to choose?

Writing to his friend, Mr Wroblewski tries to disarm the "dark riddle" that continues to plague them both: "From that distance," he urges, "the dark has no power. It has no life of its own. It is a reflection" (654). In Paris together they will "exchange visions through the afternoon and into the evening, with the lights inside the café growing brighter and brighter as the trees outside become part of the night" (644). Mr Wroblewski's visionary fantasy is comparable to his wife's delusion that there is a musician playing Schubert all night long in the neighbouring apartment. And yet the limbo in which Magda's loss of memory has stranded her is a constant warning to her husband: "She is poised on the moment between dark and light, when the last dream of dawn is shredding rapidly and awareness of morning has barely caught hold. She lives that split second all day long" (644). For both their sakes, Mr. Wroblewski must "hold to his side of the frontier between sleeping and waking" (647) for as long as he can.

Given so much darkness—the anxiety and despair of these émigrés' old age, their poverty or financial worries—and given the suspect glitter of the city's lights, what do they offer us, those ironic illuminations Gallant presents to us—the radiant paradigm of the Berlin Wall, the chinks of light proffered by the New Europe? Perhaps it is only the lessons we can draw from them, if we are capable of doing so—that the radiance stemmed from an untenable simplification of moral possibilities, and the chinks of light from self-protective blindness: that reality, with or without quotation marks, is far more complex, ambiguous, paradoxical than we can bear to admit. We can remember here those qualities of contradiction and irresolution that distinguished Adam Tremski, a Jew who may have been "a true convert" to Catholicism, or "just a writer who sometimes sounded like one," a man who "could claim one thing and its opposite in the same sentence" (629). We can also remember the consoling truth devised by Mr Wroblewski at the end of "A State of Affairs": "A sheet of black glass means nothing: it is not a cloud or the sky" (654).

Perhaps these lessons—what we remember of what has moved us—give us light enough to see by: just.

(Dis)playing Différ*a*nce

"Across the Bridge" by Mavis Gallant

Agnès Whitfield

With his characteristic penchant for linguistic subversion, Derrida uses "*différance*," deliberately spelled with an "a," to display the two meanings of the French word "différer," from the Latin "differre:"one articulated in time (to defer or temporise); the other rooted in space (to differ, to be different or to disagree). And he links both notions in a theory of language which posits the deferral and the displacement ("espacement") of meaning as constitutive of difference, or effects of difference in communication (8–9). Inevitably, words can only stand in for something absent; meaning is differed. Similarly, when they are reiterated, words cannot be truly identical to the original utterance; meaning is always in some way displaced.

This is, of course, an overly schematic representation of Derrida's complex and evolving approach to language and *différance*, but it suffices here. For my purpose is not to engage with his philosophy, but to use the connection he makes between difference, deferral and displacement to explore what I see as one of the fundamental characteristics of Mavis Gallant's writing, her own particular, and seemingly paradoxical, approach to language and difference. More precisely, my aim is to weave together two previously separate strands in critical studies of Mavis Gallant's writing: on the one hand, the demonstrated importance of deferral at various levels in her writing; and, on the other, the singularly complex and paradoxical inter-linguistic and intercultural context from which she writes as an expatriate author. Both these strands interconnect, as I hope to show, in the particular way difference is played out, or rather (dis)played, in her writing, at once revealed and deferred or displaced.

The importance of deferral in Mavis Gallant's writing is well established. Janice Kulyk Keefer has pointed out how the "impression of authorial evasion or indifference" in the tone of Gallant's work prevents "her readers from forming easy, conventional responses" (*Reading*, 42) to the situations her narrators represent. Meaning, in this perspective, is not given, but deferred, left for the reader to reconstruct. While to some degree this is always the case in fiction, in Mavis Gallant's ironic writing style, the importance of deferral is such that Keefer sees the "qualities of abstractness and detachment [as] characteris[ing] her narratives" (*Reading*, 8). Karen Smythe touches on the same characteristic of Gallant's style, when she observes that:

> Gallant portrays characters as they experience the apprehended "after-*a*ffects" of loss (rather than portraying the actual experience of loss), and so induces readers to understand that experience for themselves in the course of mimpathic [sic] involvement, in giving form to that experience outside of the story's frame of reference. (23)

For both critics, however, deferral is seen as problematic, open to difference and disagreement, resistance and dislocation. "One of the most risky aspects of choosing ironic impersonality to define narrative tone," remarks Keefer, "is the insecurity and fear it engenders in the reader" (42). "Irony both constructs and disrupts meanings," notes Smythe. It "provides the distance required by the elegist and reader to construct the model of mourning, [...] *and* to critique the very model the text represents on personal and cultural levels" (28). Whereas Keefer speaks of reader "resistance," echoing those critics who find Gallant's prose cruel, Smythe sees the reader involved in a complex process of "transferential reconstruction" (29).

A similar, double-edged use of deferral underlies Gallant's fiction on the level of theme and plot. Smythe's remarks are again pertinent. Gallant "does not often render emotional realism at the immediate point of crisis," she states, "but rather depicts the after-*a*ffects of experience, a displaced form of affect" (26). Making the same link between deferral and displacement, Neil Besner sees deferral as a form of obstinate resistance to transition: "Gallant's characters," he maintains, "are often figures on the verge of perceptions they cannot quite accommodate, or stranded beyond the end of one era, before the beginning of another" (*Light*, 48). In his view, deferral, as movement in time, leads not to resolution, but to displaced repetition:

> The most significant structural unity in Gallant's fiction is her stories' recurrent evocations of returns [...] These returns are structural figurations of Gallant's fundamental concern with time. They do not imply a cyclical repetition of history; rather they imply subtle alteration, variations within each repetition, each return to a 'locked situation.' (151)

Like deferral and displacement, difference permeates Mavis Gallant's writing with similarly problematic implications. Her characters "are almost always foreigners, travellers or guests," notes Grazia Merler, "or they feel as if they were literally or metaphorically foreign" (2). Living an "equivocal existence talking most of the time at cross-purposes," continues Merler, such characters are caught in a "hazy zone between their fantasies and reality, both refusing and accepting to acknowledge the ambiguous polyvalence of their motivations" (2). In her analysis of Gallant's "Virus X," Keefer offers a more positive view. She acknowledges that Mavis Gallant's presentation of immigrant ethnic difference is "discomforting" ("Bridges," 102), but reads it as a "critique of what has become [in Canada] the ideology of multiculturalism [:] the harmonious integration of its various immigrant communities by accommodating rather than eradicating ethno-cultural differences" (100–1). Nevertheless, in Mavis Gallant's portrayal of immigrants in Canada, as read by Keefer, there is little potential for finding identity between or within differences:

> Not bridges, but borders that turn out to be chasms—this is Gallant's iconic expression of the effects of ethno-cultural difference on hyphenated Canadians, those who do not really belong, who are made to feel like strangers in both their countries, old and new. (107)

Paradoxically, while difference in her fiction is portrayed as unyielding and unwanted, Mavis Gallant has insistently claimed and highlighted her own linguistic difference as an author. A Canadian writing in English while surrounded by French in Paris, she adamantly refuses to identify herself as a writer in exile. Nor has she attempted to transcend the linguistic gap by writing in the language of her adopted country. When asked if she had ever tried to write in French, she replied categorically: "Non. J'en suis incapable" (Girard and Valette, 81). As Judith Woodsworth has pointed out, Gallant has shown a tenacious resistance to having her books translated into French, even going so far as to contest their very translatability: "English and French, in fact, are the last two languages you can translate, she has said" (53). Geographical dislocation seems to be essential to her creativity, but in a contradictory fashion, as illustrated by her categorical statement, unusual to say the least, that should she ever write in French, she "could no longer live in France" (Zand, 24)!

Despite her more than fluent bilingualism and her choice to live her daily life in-between two languages, Mavis Gallant has clearly defined her writing in opposition to the postmodern interest in hybridity (or *métissage),* the liminal, the obscure or manifest passages between languages. In her view, languages are, on the contrary, to be kept distinctly separate from one another, all the more so if they happen to be in contact. As Keefer has pointed out, Mavis Gallant is "determined to 'keep a strong writing wall in place' to prevent not just the words but the psychological and intellectual structures of these languages from crossing boundaries: [...] 'If I were to write in French, not only would I put things differently, but I would never set out to say the same things' " (*Reading*,16).

On one level, this statement simply reflects Mavis Gallant's sensitivity to how language shapes discourse. However, how she chooses to formulate this concept is significant, and reveals a more complex personal relationship to language and difference. Her formulation echoes both the temporal deferral ("If I were to write...") and the spatial displacement ("I would never set out...") which underlie Derrida's notion of *différance*. Yet Mavis Gallant insists here not only on difference, but on a sort of reinforced *double* difference. In her view, were she to seek to attenuate her own linguistic *difference* as an English writer in Paris and work in French, she would in fact become *doubly* different, not the *same* writer writing in *another* language, but *another* writer writing in *another* language. When one thinks of how much invisible translation haunts the dialogues of her work, such a position seems particularly contradictory. What happens then when the anglophone writer transcribes the conversations of her many French characters, not in their native language, but in an English already displaced, rewritten, transformed through difference? And why is this work of translation, this unacknowledged passage from one language to another, to which Mavis Gallant curiously makes no reference, revealed yet negated in her texts, present by its product, but invisible, (dis)played?

In two separate and different types of texts, one her autobiographical preface to the recent McClelland and Stewart collection of her short stories, *The Selected Stories of Mavis Gallant*, the other, her short story, "Across the Bridge," Mavis Gallant uses strikingly similar tropes to portray her contradictory positions vis-à-vis language and difference. Other short stories and texts by Mavis Gallant can offer valuable insights into the question of *différance*, but these two texts are particularly relevant to the present discussion by their evocation of the bridge, a common metaphor in the Canadian context for translation, inter-linguistic communication and *rapprochement*. The very title of the short story (and the volume in which it appears), "Across the Bridge," is revealing. Our attention is drawn not to the passage from one side to the other, the action of crossing the bridge or translating, but to what lies on the other side. Read as a reversal of the conventional trope of the bridge, this fictional image of an undefined "other side" announces difference as requiring displacement, desired perhaps yet necessarily deferred. However, by its very indeterminacy, it leaves us paradoxically uncertain as to the direction, the advisability and even the possibility of this crossing between identity and difference. While not offering a definitive answer on writing and *différance* in Mavis Gallant's fiction, an analysis of the similarities and dissimilarities with which these two short texts present issues in language and difference can, I believe, provide important insights into how these complex questions play themselves out, or rather, (dis)play themselves in Mavis Gallant's writing.

Significantly, it is precisely with the moment of crossing that the short story starts: "We were walking over the bridge from the Place de la Concorde, my mother and I—arm in arm, like two sisters who never quarrel" (*Selected Stories*, 118). The past progressive tense in this first sentence underlines the passage, rather than the arrival, leaving the characters, and the reader, suspended, for a moment at least, on the bridge. What happens, or fails to take place, during the crossing is also relevant. Presented here with the reduced authority status of a sister, the mother of the main character, Sylvie, is carrying the invitations for her daughter's wedding to Arnaud Pons, the son of a friend of Sylvie's father. To be sent, the invitations must be franked by a cousin and friend of the latter, a deputy at the National Assembly, who "was expecting [us] at the Palais Bourbon, at the other end of the bridge" (118).

On the thematic level, crossing the bridge is linked to marriage, another common trope for the coming together of difference in the tradition of Hugh MacLennan's *Two Solitudes*. However, in Mavis Gallant's short story, the theme of marriage is, from the very beginning, set against the as yet *unbridged* and perhaps *unbridgeable* inequality in language and power which underlies difference between men and women. The bridge is presented as separating two worlds: on the Right Bank, the domestic domain where the women have their place; on the Left Bank, the world of the Father, of politics, even of discussions which "women were not expected to join in" (119). This is also the world of authority and communication in language, for the wedding has been decided upon to please the father, and the invitations will not be communicated, passed on, without, literally and symbolically, the stamp of the father, represented here by his male cousin.

Not surprisingly, given the subordinate status of the two women (the mother is described elsewhere in relation to the father as being "like a girl of fourteen" (120), the crossing itself is represented as highly problematic. The women are ill-equipped for the walk; the weather appears ominous: "It was hot on the bridge, July in April. We still wore our heavy coats. Too much good weather was not to be trusted" (119). The midpoint is fittingly underlined with vague international references to those who move between without taking root: "Halfway across, we stopped to look at a boat with strings of flags, and tourists sitting along the bank" (119). Sensing the point of no return, the unhappy young protagonist seeks refuge in flight. She thinks of painting, associated with the sky, a conventional symbol of the transcendence of individual identity: "There were no clouds over the river, but just the kind of firm blue sky I found easy to paint" (119). On the other hand, she feels a desire for the dissolution of her identity through immersion or drowning: "I stared at the water and saw how far below it was and how cold it looked, and I said, 'If I weren't a Catholic, I'd throw myself in' " (119). Death haunts her vision of marriage itself: she doesn't want to marry a young man who "makes [her] listen to records—all those stories about women dying, Brünhild, Mimi and Butterfly" (121).

It is at this point that the mother decides to abort the crossing and throws the invitations into the Seine: "She placed the leather bag on the parapet and turned it upside down over the river, using both hands. I watched the envelopes fall in a slow shower and land on the dark water and float apart" (121). In their "long shower," the white invitations echo the absent clouds in the blue sky of the protagonist's painting. Later on, they become "white patches just under the surface of the river, quite far along. They could have been candy wrappers or scraps of rubbish from a barge" (121). As paradoxical images of writing and language, the invitations are richly symbolic. Although written upon by others, they become increasingly distant and inaccessible blank pages for the protagonist herself. Fittingly, the moment, like the protagonist, is imbued with silence: "Strangers leaned on the parapet and stared, too, but nobody spoke" (121).

Painting resurfaces later on in "Across the Bridge" as an alternate means of expression. Ironically, the protagonist meets another suitor while sketching in the Luxembourg Gardens. With this suitor, Bernard Brunelle, there is even an actual exchange of letters. Language is possible, but only outside the framework of paternal authority. When confronted with her parent's demand, the protagonist remains at a loss to produce the one letter "that mentions marriage" (129) with Brunelle. "It was between the lines," she maintains; "It was nowhere" (129), concludes her mother.

As Sylvie's wedding to Bernard Brunelle retreats into fantasy, so, too, is painting threatened, albeit in an ambiguous fashion: "I promise never to paint pictures again" she declares, almost unconsciously, in a remark that "said itself" (129). As her rebellion fades and she returns to her father's choice, Arnaud Pons, the sky blue of her painting breaks down into two separate, yet equally trivialised, strands. The "faded blue" (131) of the family name on their storefront in Nice, and the "pale blue" of her mother's dress "for the wrong season" (132) come to represent the nostalgic blue of a far-removed childhood, linked to a somewhat dysfunctional mother. At the same time, her penchant for artistic fantasy literally dissolves into smoke. In the restaurant where she and Arnaud confirm their reconciliation, she observes "a flat layer of thin blue smoke" (140) floating above three young women: "Once I was married, [she] thought, I would smoke. It would give me something to do with my hands when other people talked" (140). In both cases, one displacement of expression, from language to art, leads to another, in a continued movement of deferral.

The temporal and spatial configuration of the trope of the bridge functions in a similar manner to portray Sylvie's ambiguous movement towards resigned acceptance of her father's wish, to which her mother, too, finally accedes. The temporal quality of the past progressive in the first sentence of the short story places the passage over the bridge in the timelessness of what is unfinished, endlessly deferred. This impression is heightened by the fact that the arrival of the women "across the bridge" is never recounted. Four pages on, after flashbacks about the family, we are still walking with mother and daughter on the bridge, their "cousin, still waiting in his office" (121). Only one sentence, whose relationship with the narrative present of the protagonist is quite ambiguous ("In the end, she said the wedding had to be postponed owing to a death in Arnaud's family" [121]), allows us to surmise that the two women must indeed have reached the Left Bank, and the cousin waiting there to frank the invitations.

The plot takes the protagonist once more across the bridge, for the reconciliation with Arnaud, whom she is to meet at the old Montparnasse train station. This time, her father drives her there, but the bridge itself is absent from the narrative. After their meeting, Sylvie decides to walk home: "it was a long way, much of it uphill, once I crossed the river" (143). The rain and the "sculptured" "gray clouds" (143) that accompany her recall the absent clouds and the "shower" of invitations of the initial scene. On this return from the Left Bank to the Right Bank, the bridge is again absent. The narrative leaves the protagonist still on the Left Bank, on her way, not to the bridge, but to the river: "I turned the corner and started down toward the Seine, walking slowly" (143). Use of the present participle echoes the past progressive of the initial sentence; the protagonist is left "walking," not away from, but back towards the bridge she started on.

The effect of this confusing narrative structure is to (dis)play the positioning of the protagonist. If she is now in fact "across the bridge," she has not arrived there under her own steam, nor does she seem destined to remain there. As a trope of *rapprochement* and access to difference, the crossing of the bridge is omitted from the narrative; the direction is reversed, and ultimately, the movement towards appropriation of the language of the father rendered ambiguous. This ambiguity is reinforced thematically, the protagonist continuing to perceive her relationship with

Arnaud as a form of drowning. As she listens to his operas with him, she sees herself in the water: "I would shut my eyes and let myself fall. A still surface of water rose to meet me. I was not dying but letting go" (128). Although Arnaud has informed her "You would have all summer long for your art. I would never stand in your way" (142), we have already seen the blue image linked with art go up in "smoke." It seems unlikely that Sylvie, letting herself go in a form of creative drowning, will once again pick up her paint brushes. Rather, her relation to expression and language remains in deferral, represented by an indeterminate series of repeated displacements. The crossing itself is (dis)played, represented but aborted, displaced literally below or above the bridge, deferred indefinitely in the flow of the water or the drifting of the echoing blue sky.

These same tropes of bridge, river, banks, sky, writing, and painting, as well as their symbolic evocation of displacement and deferral, reappear in the author's autobiographical preface to her *Selected Stories*. As if to answer the question, *why do you write?*, Mavis Gallant starts by recalling Georges Bernanos' description of writing as being "like rowing a boat out to sea: The shoreline disappears, it is too late to turn back, and the rower becomes a galley slave" (ix). As Gallant makes it her own, however, the image shifts from sea to river, and the writer ceases to exist separately, the rower above the waves becoming one with the water itself: "I have lived in writing, like a spoonful of water in a river, for more than forty-five years" (ix). While positively portrayed here, further along in the preface, the image shifts again slightly, moving back to the rower, perhaps, but now reflecting a certain impatience: "I still do not know what impels anyone sound of mind to leave dry land and spend a lifetime describing people who do not exist" (x). Finally, in a direct echo of the drowning which tempts the protagonist of "Across the Bridge," it is linked to moving across a bridge, and more specifically to two emotionally trying returns to Montreal, the city of Mavis Gallant's childhood.

The first occurs when she was eighteen, "and hoped no one would notice. A few people in Montreal believed I had died. It was a rumor, a floating story with no setting or plot" (xi). Fifty years later, she returns to Châteauguay, a small town across the Saint Lawrence river, on the South Shore, where she had spent summers and two whole winters as a child with both her parents. She is again haunted by the image of a drowned child. In both instances, the image is displaced, attributed not to the writer's own memory, but to the memory of others. Transposed, in the first case, into the language of fiction ("a floating story,") it is linked in the later return to the vague, almost mythic memory of the young descendent of a former neighbour: "He knew about our house, so radically modified now, because of some child, a girl, who had lived there a long time before and been drowned in the river" (xii). Mavis Gallant never contacts the great-aunt of the young man, as he encourages her to do. There is no direct communication with the past: "I never called. There was nothing to ask. Another English Canadian family with just one child had lived on the same side of the river. They had a large house, with a stone wall around it, and the drowned child was a boy" (xii). Clearly, the author herself is no more in danger of drowning. Yet the evocation of an untimely death lingers on. Something vaguely ominous continues to cling at once to the act of writing fiction and to its metaphorical movement over (or rather through) the river.

Structurally, the spatial configuration of the autobiographical narrative of Mavis Gallant's second trip home, as recounted in the Preface, is almost identical with Sylvie's aborted crossing of the Seine, and equally ambiguous. The author starts by recalling, not the return to Châteauguay which is the apparent object of the narrative, but rather her last departure from Châteauguay across the Saint Lawrence to Montreal: "I came back to Châteauguay fifty years after taking the Montreal train for the last time, across the bridge, over the river" (xi); and she goes on to recall first not Châteauguay but Montreal. As in the short story, the "left" or south bank of the river is associated with the father. Châteauguay is clearly heavily charged emotionally for the author: "I would never have returned alone to Châteauguay. It was the last place where we had lived as a family" (xi), before the death of her father.

When Mavis Gallant crossed the Saint Lawrence river from the North to the South shore to revisit Châteauguay where she had spent her summers as a child, was she reminded of crossing the Seine from the Right to the Left Bank in her adopted home? Does the topography of Paris offer subconscious affinities to that of Montreal? Certainly the height and width of the Champlain bridge have nothing in common with the friendly human dimensions of the historic bridges over the Seine, but its majesty does echo the intense power of childhood memories to separate and hurt. Deferred for fifty years, its telling displaced, her crossing to Châteauguay, like Sylvie's trip out onto the Parisian bridge, is a fragile undertaking, not to be accomplished "alone." "Composed of strangers, largely indifferent, intent on getting the assignment over and a flight home" (xi), the television crew which accompanies the author recalls, by its transience, the tourists on the quays of the Seine. "Their indifference was what I needed," writes Mavis Gallant, "a thick glass wall against the effects of memory" (xi).

In the Preface, painting is also associated with the masculine, and presented, like drowning, as a form of displaced access to expression. This time, the image of art is doubly displaced, linked first to the figure of the author's father, an amateur painter, and second, to his displacement from Europe to Canada. Although, in the judgement of his daughter, he was destined only to be a "dedicated amateur," this displacement, in Gallant's perspective, was nonetheless "required" by his ideal: "In a sense, he never started out, except along a path of some firm ideal concerning life and art. The ideality required displacement; he went from England to Canada" (x). A misleading, fictitious displacement also marked his death for the writer: "When my father died, I was told he had gone to England, and would be back before long" (xi).

It would be presumptuous to reach any definitive conclusions from this analysis of two short texts by Mavis Gallant. The structural similarities in the way both texts position artistic expression and *différance* with respect to the trope of the bridge are nonetheless remarkable. Both texts (dis)play the conventional image of the bridge as a means of joining two languages or crossing from one to the other. The act of crossing is alluded to, yet not represented, endlessly deferred or displaced. Both texts also superimpose on the bridge as trope of linguistic difference, a split between gender connections, between the language of the mother and that of the father.

In "Across the Bridge," the status of the mother tongue is that of a sister tongue, without power. The sisters who "never quarrel" in the first sentence will be separated, literally and symbolically through Sylvie's marriage, by the father's desire, without ensuring access for Sylvie to the male world "across the bridge." The fundamental inequality between mother and father tongue will remain unbridged, if not unbridgeable. In Mavis Gallant's autobiographical text, the mother/father topographical distinction is more complex, but nonetheless similar. "I was taught the alphabet three times" (xvii), she writes. The Island of Montreal (positioned as the Right Bank) is associated both with French, which she learns at four years of age as a boarder in a French convent school, and with English, whose alphabet her father teaches her. French surfaces here as a possible but only partially endowed mother tongue. References to her mother are not connected to language, while her grandmother expresses incomprehension at the decision to send her granddaughter to a French convent school. As in the short story, the Left Bank is clearly associated with English as the father tongue; in Châteauguay she also attends an English-language school for the first time. The association is doubly painful, however. At school, she is made fun of because of her French accent. She officially learns the alphabet for the third time, disappointedly concluding "whatever it was, it could never be sung" (xviii). More importantly, Châteauguay is linked to the death of her Father, and the "flawed legacy, a vocation without the competence to sustain it" which has "haunted [her] from early youth" (xii).

Like the bridge as a trope of rapprochement, linguistic difference as gendered identity is (dis)played, shown but dislocated. In this case, it is not the act of crossing over itself that is deferred and displaced, but the identity of each shore. In both texts, access to the language "across the bridge," the language of the father, is uncertain (desire is ambivalent), while the mother tongue, due to social norms or a particular family context, is in some way undervalued or disabled. The effect is to present both gendered languages as being in some way ineffectual, insufficient, untrustworthy, not to be identified with completely. This uncertainty of identity is accentuated by the manner in which both texts position English and French as mother tongues, in the sense of native language. Examined together, these texts (dis)play the habitual position attributed to Mavis Gallant's two languages, suggesting that English, and not French, is the language of the "other," waiting "across the bridge." This is the case symbolically in the Preface, and literally in the short story where English is (dis)played as the language of the father, in the absence of any visible translation of French. Finally, in a direct reversal of Mavis Gallant's insistence on maintaining a wall between French and English, both texts situate access to language as a form of artistic expression in the space under or over the bridge, between the two shores of difference. In this space, the boundaries are fluid, highly mobile, yet no less problematic. Art is experienced as a loss of identity, a form of drowning, or ephemeral, liable to disappear in a wisp of smoke. "What fiction is about," Gallant has stated elsewhere, not without a hint of bitterness, "is that something is taking place and that nothing lasts" (*Paris Notebooks*, 177).

In the Preface, Mavis Gallant presents her childhood acquisition of English and French as an inconvenient doubling, "two systems of behaviour," "two environments," "two codes of social behaviour" (xv), reminiscent of the double difference she associates with writing in French. In the framework of Derrida's sense of *différance*, this repetition of difference cannot lead to the equivalence of two identities; each repetition automatically carries with it some form of displacement and deferral; two different shores are created. From this perspective, her apparently paradoxical statement that, were she to write in French, she "would never set out" in the same way is completely logical. The direction of the crossing would in fact be reversed. However, this interpretation cannot explain why, to pursue the conventional trope of the bridge, she would become, by so doing, *another* writer. The answer to this paradox lies in the much more complex relationship to language that is revealed by how she (dis)plays difference.

Commenting on the importance of the "paradoxical nature of time" in Gallant's writing, Neil Besner touches on this when he concludes that "there is no direction home because there is insufficient sense of where home is" (*Light*,152). By (dis)playing the crossing, evoking the passage between languages, only to defer and displace the arrival "across the bridge," Mavis Gallant acknowledges both the desire for home (identity), and its absence. Similarly, her focus on social and political realities, associated with the male world, by (dis)playing the emotional dimension conventionally associated with the feminine, evokes this absence, leaving the reader, as Smythe observes, to cross the bridge, to reconstruct the after or prior *a*ffects of events. In this respect, each shore is paradoxically the same in that neither can sustain identity. To be an effective destination, one, at least, would have to be truly ''different.'' It is this particular experience of *différance*, difference desired but deferred and dislocated, that is (dis)played in Mavis Gallant's seemingly paradoxical insistence on her double linguistic codes, on the fact that were she to write in French, she would be doubly *different*. Because each language is insufficient, literally and symbolically wanting, writing can only take place in-between: "Somewhere in this duality," writes Mavis Gallant in the Preface, in a statement that is to be understood literally, "may be the exact point of the beginning of writing" (xv). From this perspective, her desire to maintain a firm wall between her two languages is perfectly understandable. This space in-between, under or over the bridge, can only be claimed if the shores are kept firmly in place. And in a final Derridean irony, one of the very attractions of this otherwise uncertain space for language in-between identities, is that, like the transience of tourists or communicators passing through, it allows for *in*difference.

Mavis Gallant's Fiction

Taking the (Rhetorical) Measure of the Turning Point

Marta Dvorak

In her essay "What Is Style?", which appeared shortly after the publication of *Home Truths*, the collection of short stories on which I shall be basing my textual analysis, Mavis Gallant argues that fiction involves making a statement, which is simply that "something is taking place and that nothing lasts" (6). She explains that

> [a]gainst the sustained tick of a watch, fiction takes the measure of a life, a season, a look exchanged, the turning point, desire as brief as a dream, the grief and terror that after childhood we cease to express. (6)

In this instance, she is writing literary theory, but the very technique of her critical remarks, with their seemingly chaotic enumeration of disparate components, their yoking of abstract, concrete, sensory, affective and intellectual elements, echoes the style of her fictional writing. The apparent disorder of the components suggests the pointillist manner of modernists writers such as Katherine Mansfield or Ernest Buckler, or of postmodernists like Timothy Findley, whose phenomenological and subjective textual approaches present similarities with Mavis Gallant's. These are writers who in small impressionistic brush-strokes capture what language cannot describe otherwise. Mansfield is well-known for her pictorial descriptions, while Buckler's prose is studded with descriptions suggesting correspondences between the precise and complex patterns of a snowflake or a daisy, and a divine plan or perfect cosmic design. In *The Wars* notably, Findley too functions like a painter, capturing with small touches fragments of perception, bits of reality that are like the old photographs that crumble in the hands of the narrator trying to piece the story together.

In her book on Katherine Mansfield, and more specifically in the chapter entitled "Some Basic Aesthetics of Literary Impressionism," Julia Van Gunsteren argues that

> Literary Impressionists, like the Impressionists in painting, focused on perception. They attempted to formulate reality by breaking it into momentary fragments, selected intuitively and subjectively. They relied on sensory (ap)perceptions, used clusters of images and rendered their emotions in a ''slice of life'' picture of some everyday, ordinary experience. (55)

She argues that the "confused colliding of sensations, impressions and experiences" of these Literary Impressionists are produced by "[l]ittle touches [...] placed side by side" (55), and generated through the prevalence of accumulation and concatenation. These "clusters of images" are the very groundwork of Gallant's texts, which are non-linear, multi-layered, multi-dimensional, multi-genre constructions shifting among the modes of narrative, essay,[1] fictional autobiography, and satire. The author's temporal strategies often involve a double, or even triple temporal dimension, the diegetic events told in the preterite interspersed with narratorial comments and value judgments in the present tense. The focalization in the Linnet Muir sequence, to take but one well-known example, shifts constantly. There is the point of view of the narrat*ed* I at different moments of her development—as a naive child discovering her cultural environment and the world of words, and as a young adult discovering the world of work and the world of writing. These alternating points of view and accompanying leaps in time are in turn crisscrossed with the voice of the older self-conscious narrat*ing* I, whose comments and evaluations are woven into the textual fabric throughout. In one simple sentence from "Voices Lost in Snow," "I *felt* and *am* certain I *have* not *invented* Georgie's disappointment at not seeing Angus alone" (291; emphases mine unless signaled otherwise), the author, with the juxtaposition of preterite, present, and present perfect tenses, telescopes seeing and telling separated by decades. Also contributing to the layering effect of the text is the writer's trademark use of the ironic mode, for irony by definition is the simultaneous actualization of two levels of meaning, a literal one that is denoted or explicit, and another one that is connoted, created through certain mechanisms of derivationé. By in/verting the usual semantic levels, by giving the connoted, or latent, precedence over the denoted, or stated, Gallant sub/verts meaning, pointing beyond what Hutcheon might term "the slippery nature of language," to "the incongruities of our culture and our society at large" (*Splitting*, 28).

But if irony is discourse with a double meaning, a signifier with two signifieds, it does not constitute the only group of signs in Gallant's texts with doubled meanings. Neil Besner is quite right in asserting that the "slice of life" interpretation—suggested, we have seen, by critics like Van Gunsteren—needs to be tempered in the light of the indirect language of literature as posited by Roland Barthes, who argues that literature names *things* in detail so as to suggest *concepts:*

> La première condition de la littérature, c'est, paradoxalement, d'accomplir un langage indirect: nommer en détail les choses afin de ne pas nommer leur sens dernier et tenir cependant sans cesse ce sens menaçant, désigner le monde comme un répertoire de signes dont on ne dit pas ce qu'ils signifient. («La Bruyère,» 232)[2]

In essence, naming the object alone makes it possible not to limit the sign to a single meaning, but allows it to resonate in a fertile way, or, to use Barthes's poetic term, to "tremble" [3]. Gallant's "clusters of images", like her irony, serve in an indirect fashion to designate a second meaning: they are Gallant's "turning points" or what Hutcheon might term "splitting images." I shall attempt to demonstrate how, through the rhetorical device of accumulation, these clusters of images produce the dynamics of displacement or disjunction, with the ultimate purpose of moving in other directions and of generating new meaning.

The process can be detected in the opening paragraph of "Orphans' Progress," which begins *in medias res*, at the crucial point in the narrative when the two small sisters have been ripped out of the cocoon of their francophone, maternal environment and placed into an anglophone, also female but patriarchal one. The dynamics are hermeneutic, for the reader immediately encounters both proleptic and analeptic reconstruction-inviting structures. The first sentence projects us back by opening out onto a pre-text, "When the Collier girls were six and ten they were taken away from their mother," while the last sentence, "What they *remembered afterwards* of their grandmother was goat's milk, goat eyes, and the frightened man" (56), projects us both forward and back, to a point already in the past for the extradiegetic narrator, but in the future still to come for the protagonists, a future in which "present event" ("They went to school in Ontario *now*"—a space between two deaths) will have been transformed into "past memory".[4]

The apparently chaotic enumeration, ternary in structure, is the closure to an apologue—an anecdote or tale that writers make use of to illustrate some underlying truth, to amplify an idea:

> Their grandmother was scrupulous about food, particularly for these underfed children, and made them drink goat's milk. Two goats bought specially to supply the orphans were taken by station wagon to a buck fifty miles away, the girls accompanying them for reasons of enlightenment. A man in a filling station was frightened by the goats, because of their oblong eyes. The girls were not reflected in the goats' eyes, as they were in each other's. What they remembered afterwards of their grandmother was goat's milk, goat eyes, and the frightened man. (56)

The parataxis foregrounds the apologue's quasi-allegorical function. The paratactic erasure of discursive segments indicating syntactic relationships reflects visually on the space of the page the rubbing out of the relationship with the mother. It announces the erasure of the bonding, of the affective comfort and physical warmth underscored by the device of dislocation in the later statement, "They slept in the same bed, all three" (57), the intimate organic warmth of the bed to be replaced by the inhospitable "freezing" linoleum (*i.e.*, non-organic, un-natural) floor of the paternal grandmother (58). The dysphoric lexical field of constraint, repulsion and fear contributes to generating what the rhetorician Henri Morier calls the *noema*, the theme or moral. Although none of the terms taken individually is a symbol in itself, the whole apologue functions structurally like a simile or extended comparison, and is meant to be interpreted symbolically. If Gallant resorts to the device of the apologue, it is because she knows that it constitutes an excellent vehicle for conveying meaning of an emotional or ethical nature. The associations and connections the receiver is intended to make are suggested through the small brush strokes of concretization—the oblong vs human eyes, the absence/presence of reflection, the concatenation or repetition of the goats' eyes, the goats' milk, all replacing the expression of abstract ideas. The devices of enumeration and concatenation, and the mood that they generate, are evocative of Ernest Buckler's technique of hypnotic litanies, which the author himself explained are synecdochic in function, creating a network of interconnections, producing relationships of inclusion and "whole fields of implication." In a letter to his editor at Knopf, he argued that the device underlines

> the omnipresence of the far in the near, the universal in the particular, the macrocosm in the microcosm, the duplicate rendering of every mood in some physical object or cast of nature, the translatability of the senses one into another, the inter-locking and cross-pollination of all things tangible or intangible.[5]

In the same way, Gallant's final, haunting, oneiric enumeration reinforces the exemplary dimension of her anecdote. She too realizes that the rhetorical device serves to connect the abstract and the concrete, the general and the particular. Jakobson, after all, Dupriez reports (158), sees it as the exposure of the paradigm, outside the function of communication, pointing out that whether it be the inventory aspiring to exhaustivity, or the partial enumeration serving as an *exemplum*, it is noteworthy for its capacity to display something in a small space—particularly appropriate for the economic genre of the short story.

As an *exemplum*, a mode of concretization in which animals habitually represent the qualities of the human world, Gallant's passage illustrates rather than demonstrates, and the receiver carries away a powerful impression of terror, powerlessness, and alienation. It paves the way for the pathos of the concluding sentences of the short story. The sisters who have only each other, who are reflected only in each other's eyes, are finally estranged. The *excipit* notably multiplies references to vision, to the gaze, to show that now Cathie is no longer reflected in her sister's eyes—she has been erased:

> "*Look*, Mildred," said her [adopted] father, and let the car slow down on a particular street. The parents *craned* at a garage, and at dirty-legged children with torn sneakers on their feet. Mildred *glanced up* and then *back* at her book. She had no reason to believe she had *seen* it before, or would ever [*see* it] again. (62; emphases mine)

The underlying unifying *noema,* or theme, of Gallant's accumulated ''little touches'' is an implicit indictment of what Margaret Atwood terms "power politics,"and which in an interview with Jan Castro, she defines as "all paradigms of dominance and subservience" (Van Spanckeren, 223), and which she explores in *The Handmaid's Tale*:

> Maybe none of this is about control. Maybe it isn't really about who can own whom, who can do what to whom and get away with it, even as far as death. (144)

Children and milk, a ride in a car, a man in a filling station—in this *incipit*, we can see at work the "slice of life" technique with its fragments of sensory perceptions. These fragments, in their implication, go beyond Van Gunsteren's suggested formulation of visible or tangible reality, and metaphorically formulate the abstract, terrifying reality of the powerless. The text focuses indeed on a moment, "a season, a look exchanged," denoting little, but connoting all "the grief and terror that after childhood we cease to express."

Gallant takes "the measure of a life, a season" thanks to "the duplicate rendering of every mood in some physical object or cast of nature," as Buckler puts it.[6] The resulting textual web of ramifications, the cross network of analogies, take on the shape of a whole cloth, through the winding thread of concatenation. Let us look at one paragraph describing this period in the children's lives:

> *They did not know*, and never once asked, why they had been taken away. When the new social worker said to Cathie, "Were you disturbed because your mother was unhappy?" Cathie said, "She wasn't." When the girls were living with their mother, *they knew* that sometimes she listened and sometimes could not hear; nevertheless, she was there. They slept in the same bed, all three. Even when she sat on the side of the bed with her head hanging and her undone jagged-cut hair hiding her eyes [...] the children were close to her and *did not know* they were living under what would be called later "unsheltered conditions." *They never knew, until told*, that they were uneducated and dirty and in danger. [...] *They did not know, until they were told*, that they had never been properly fed. (57–58; emphases mine)

We remark the minor parallelisms of *when* [...] *when* [...] *even when* and of *sometimes* [...] *sometimes*, as well as the insistent use of polysyndeton in the series "uneducated and dirty and in danger." But the main components of the unifying concatenation involve the notions of truth, knowledge, and power. The repetition in all its variants of the series *They did not know/ they never knew/ they knew*, as well as the interplay between the active *ask* and the passive *told*, contrasts the plenitude and power of the girls' former position as subjects when living with their mother (*they knew*), with the notion of absence and their status of powerless objects, empty receptacles to be filled with imparted (and therefore biased or questionable) information (*until told/ until they were told*). But the hypnotic, musical effect of the repetitions weaving in and out not only unifies the textual fabric, but also creates a mood, a poetic, metaphorical vision.

Mavis Gallant is well known for working in the ironic mode of double discourse. But the apologues or *exempla* we have looked at, forms of symbolic narrative, are an illustration of the fact that her writing is also profoundly imaged and metaphorical. The passage I have examined revolves around the use of *objective correlatives*—a set of objects and a chain of events that are a configuration of emotions. An *exemplum* is a characteristic device of concretization, as are in many cases similes, metaphors, metonymies and synecdoches. The metaphor after all is a trope that, like irony, generates double vision, for by replacing one signifier with another, it produces symbolic relationships between the signifieds. As Paul Ricoeur argues in *La Métaphore vive*, the metaphor allows the reader to see one thing under the aspect of another, or to see together, in the same category, what the ordinary gaze does not or cannot associate. It has long been attributed a simple ornamental function, associated even by traditional rhetoric with only one of the three functions of language, which are, as Michel Le Guern reminds us, *docere*, *placere*, and *movere* (to teach, please, and move or persuade). Imagery, and notably the metaphor, has been relegated to the art of pleasing, the aesthetic function of language. But imagery is far from being a decorative afterthought colouring the discourse or clothing the thought, as Mavis Gallant herself points out when she declares "what style is *not*":

> It is not a last-minute addition to prose, a charming and universal slipcover, a coat of paint used to mask the failings of a structure. ("Style," 6)

Gallant goes on to add that style is "part of the conformation of whatever the author has to say." What we shall see is how the metaphor in Gallant's texts does serve to persuade or move the receiver, and how it ultimately allows the writer to name realities for which language has no proper term.

Gallant senses that the metaphor is more powerful than the simile, for we can see with an example taken from "Varieties of Exile" how she turns simile into metaphor and then goes on to extend the metaphor. In an essay-like passage (*docere*) denouncing the abuses of authoritarianism in all its forms, from the small social unit of the family to the large geopolitical unit of the Empire, the narrator focuses on the plight of an individual, Frank Cairns, whose name, true to the device of antonomasia, is representative of a collective category—that of the Remittance Man. These remittance men have been banished to Commonwealth countries by their English upper-class families for economic or moral reasons, and are sent a small annual stipend on condition that they not return to England. The narrator makes the following comparison:

> They were like children waiting for the school vacation so that they could go home, except that at home nobody wanted them: the nursery had been turned into a billiards room and Nanny dismissed. (268)

The simile's comparison between remittance men and children packed off to boarding school, both groups unwanted by their families, remains within the logical sphere of communication. The receiver is free to admit or to contest the reasoning behind the analogy. But the simile is transformed into a metaphor (the nursery symbolizing parental nurture and protection) and the metaphor contains the dynamics of a subjective, emotional interpretation that, as Michel Le Guern points out in *Sémantique de la métaphore et de la métonymie*, cannot be easily refuted—corresponding to *movere*, the function of persuading or moving the receiver. The metaphor here is furthermore extended to underscore the irrevocable quality of the situation. It concretizes in space and time the abstract concept of banishment, generating simultaneously derision for these unproductive, immature, and irresponsible elements of society, as well as pathos for these "children" who will never grow up, who can never go home, for whom vacation-time will never come round.

If Frank Cairns triggers contradictory emotions, it is because he evokes, even represents, all the contradictions and ambiguities of the period's political, social and cultural currents of thought. Gallant conveys all the implications of the notions of synthesis and of tension between the components through another extended metaphor functioning by means of concretization:

> What Frank Cairns was to me was a curio cabinet. I took everything out of the cabinet, piece by piece, examined the objects, set them down. (275)

At other times, the writer resorts to proportional metaphorical terms, the proportional metaphor being more complex than the metaphor based on resemblance. Let us look at how the narrator deflates what Frank Cairns emulates—in this case the Fabian Society and its cautious approach to socialist reform:

> His Webbs and his Fabians were plodding and gray. I saw the men with thick moustaches, wearing heavy boots, sharing lumpy meals with moral women. (274)

An analogy is made between socialism and working class vestimentary and alimentary habits, setting up a multilateral system of relations in which heavy boots are to Fabians what indigestible food is to virtuous women. The equivalences go beyond the common logic of language in its communicational, informational function (*docere*), and by evoking multiple sensory perceptions, set up a network of subjective, emotional resonances (*movere*) centred on the narrator but inviting the connivance of the narratee. The complexity of the metaphor is reinforced by the complexity of the irony it carries. For along with the intended verbal irony of the young adult narrat*ed* I that is being transmitted, there is the structural irony inherent in the association the younger narrator makes between a movement championed by intellectuals, artists and writers like George Bernard Shaw, and stodgy, uncouth proletarianism. The amused distance the young Linnet places between herself and the "plodding" socialists finds a parallel in the amused distance[7] the older, more experienced narrator places between herself and her fiery, categorical younger self priding herself on being an intellectual revolutionary, fascinated by everything Russian or exotic, and romantically interested in refugees only so long as they did not start "eating cornflakes" (281). The proportional metaphor reflecting the point of view of the younger Linnet is deflected from its ironic target, and thanks to the visibly stereotypical notions that it carries, illustrates the older narrator's confession that at this point in time, she projected onto the world "the twilit Socialist-literary landscape of [her] reading and [her] desires" (261). The metaphor is thus a vehicle for what is ultimately a meditation on the brief moment that is youth, on its endearing tempestuousness, thoughtlessness, and zeal.

Reinforcing Gallant's metaphorical writing striving for a new or full vision, are other rhetorical devices carrying strategies of displacement, like the hypallage announcing the "black angry day" (268) on which the father pronounces the banished young man's doom. To understand the full extent of the function, we have only to look at another example from "Voices Lost in Snow," in which the narrator evokes memories of being trapped as a child in interminable adult conversations in hotel tearooms:

> (Oh, those shut-in velvet-draped unaired low-voice problems!) compensated for by creamy bitter hot chocolate poured out of a pink-and-white china pot. (293)

We can see how the hypallage, which transposes the natural relationship between two elements in a syntactic unit, renders the mood tangible by projecting the sensual qualities of the physical environment—the enclosed airless tearoom—onto the abstract arcane ideas that are being discussed there. The epithetical style, the hypnotic accumulation of qualifiers of taste and touch as well as of sight and sound, and in particular the accumulation of compounds, enhance the effect by contributing to fusing the palpable and the visual, jolting the reader into seeing with the fresh vision of a child. As is often the case with Gallant's skilful discursive techniques, in these quick brush-strokes, the portrayal of that brief moment of a child's *goûter*, the narrative gives a voice to the powerless, or to those on the peripheries of power—in this instance, children, who must endure in silence.

Also carrying a strategy of displacement, jarring the receiver into a different framework, but once again catalyzed by a questioning of contemporary society's power structure, is the zeugma, an atypical yoking of disparate elements, often an abstract and a concrete one. In "Varieties of Exile," as was seen, the young adult narrator pokes fun at Frank Cairns, the character who, being the banished black sheep of an upper-class family, represents British left-wing paternalistic concern towards the poor. She notably singles out Frank's contradictions, all stemming from the stereotypes generated by class thinking: he believes that fighting for social change is vital, but that improving the material conditions of the poor will ultimately get them nowhere, that the poor in any case all possess the strange secret of happiness. The narrator reports:

> I wondered if he really believed that a man *with no prospects and no teeth in his head* was spiritually better off than Frank Cairns, and why, in that case, Frank Cairns did not let him alone with his underfed children and his native good nature. (274)

The forced association of the abstract and concrete terms, linking poverty with decrepitude and toothlessness, foregrounds and undermines the self-congratulatory paternalistic dimension of certain currents of mid-century Socialist thinking. The zeugma tackles an ontological antithesis, deflates in an instant a romantic vision of the world, of human nature and of existing social structures, and re-establishes a certain balance.

Humanity's original relationship to texts, as Michel Foucault has pointed out in *Les Mots et les choses*, was identical to its relationships to things, consisting in both cases in perceiving, decoding and interpreting signs and their correspondences. This symbolic perception of the world as a cipher is present in Gallant's texts, which are both cipher and hermeneutic instruments with which to read and interpret the cipher of the world. The writer's rhetorical and discursive techniques interconnect the domains of perception and imagination, allowing her hermeneutic prose to take the measure of a life, a season, to find the turning point that transforms our perception of the world. Mavis Gallant is one of those writers who, as she puts it in the Preface to her collected stories, "come into the world with overlapping vision of things seen and things as they might be seen" (xv).

Notes

1. The Linnet Muir stories are shot through with aphorisms worthy of a great essayist, such as the maxim proffered in "Between Zero and One": "there are two races, those who tread on people's lives, and the others" (244).
2. "The first condition of literature is, paradoxically, setting up an *indirect* language: naming things in detail so as not to name their last or definitive meaning, yet keeping the meaning forever looming, designating the world as a repertory of signs without saying what they signify" (my translation).
3. Barthes argues: "le sens de l'objet tremble toujours, non celui du concept" ("the meaning of the object constantly trembles, while the meaning of the concept does not") (232).
4. The blurring and confusion are enhanced by a second double temporal projection: forward, when the narrator announces "Their grandmother died when the girls were seven and eleven," and immediately back again, when the story is repositioned in the pre-death "now" (56–57). The shifts also foreground the ephemerality of the moment, and are reminders that "something is taking place and that nothing lasts."
5. Buckler, Letter to Angus Cameron, 10 February 1968. Buckler Manuscript Collection, Thomas Fisher Rare Book Library, University of Toronto, Toronto.
6. "Supplementary Answers to Author's Questionnaire," sent by Buckler to his publisher, Buckler Manuscript Collection. The Questionnaire is undated, but certain references clearly situate it around the publication of his fictional memoir, *Ox Bells and Fireflies* (1968).
7. In countless examples of the device of *parenthesis*, the older narrator intervenes to confess the ignorance, naiveté, and categorical value judgments of her younger, ''green'' narrated self: "Nationalist pigheadedness [...] was known to me only on Canadian terms, and I did not always recognize its symptoms"; "older than anyone—which might have meant forty-two"; "He produced Housman and Hardy (I could not read either)" (.261, 272, 274 respectively).

Table ronde sur la traduction des oeuvres de Mavis Gallant

Canadian Cultural Centre, Paris, March 19, 1999

Participants: *Agnès Whitfield (AW), modératrice, Nicole Côté (NC), Geneviève Doze (GD), Mavis Gallant (MG), Jane Koustas (JK), Pierre-Edmond Robert (P-ER).*

AW: C'est un grand plaisir pour moi d'animer cette table ronde, avec la participation de deux traducteurs de l'oeuvre de Mavis Gallant, des critiques de la réception française de Mavis Gallant et des spécialistes de son oeuvre. Comme vous vous en doutez, il sera beaucoup question de traduction pendant la table ronde. Je commencerai par présenter les participants. Ensuite nous aborderons un certain nombre de questions.

Je commencerai par nos deux traducteurs, qui sont à la fois traducteurs et lecteurs. À ma droite, Geneviève Doze, qui est une authentique bilingue. Elle a passé une partie de son enfance en Angleterre, où elle s'est éprise de la langue et de la culture anglaises. Elle a traduit deux recueils de nouvelles de Mavis Gallant. Je vous donne les titres en français: *De l'autre côté du pont*, publié chez Fayard en 1994, et *Poisson d'avril*, publié aussi par Fayard en 1995.

À ma gauche, Pierre-Edmond Robert, qui est aussi traducteur de Mavis Gallant. *Rue de Lille* paraît en 1988, *Les Quatre Saisons*, traduction du recueil *From The Fifteenth District*, paraît en 1989. Pierre-Edmond Robert est également professeur à la Sorbonne Nouvelle. Il s'intéresse notamment à Proust—on aura l'occasion de l'entendre parler de Proust tout à l'heure. Pierre-Edmond est aussi romancier, auteur notamment d'un livre publié chez Flammarion qui s'intitule *Port Shelby*.

Nicole Côté, aussi à ma gauche, est professeure de littérature québécoise et de traduction à l'Université de Regina, en Saskatchewan, et également traductrice. Nicole a été finaliste du prix du gouverneur général pour sa traduction des nouvelles de Jane Urquhart. Elle a aussi soutenu une thèse de doctorat, à l'Université Laval, sur l'oeuvre de Jane Urquhart, du point de vue de la stylistique. C'est une contribution à l'étude de cette écrivaine canadienne-anglaise, bien connue en France.

En revenant donc à ma droite, Jane Koustas, professeur de littérature québécoise à l'Université Brock, à Saint-Catherine's, en Ontario. Jane se trouve, un peu comme moi, à cheval sur la littérature québécoise et la traduction. Elle s'intéresse beaucoup à la réception française d'auteurs canadiens-anglais et à la réception anglaise d'auteurs québécois. Elle traverse les frontières de cette façon-là. Elle dirige aussi le programme d'études canadiennes à l'Université Brock; elle est ici de par sa connaissance de la réception française de l'oeuvre de Mavis Gallant.

On a beaucoup écrit sur le style de Mavis Gallant. Gracia Merler a dit notamment de ses nouvelles: "They are written in a terse quick style that echoes the humor, the human understanding, and the curious questioning that are still the key to Mavis Gallant's work and to the characters in perpetual flux that she creates" (1). Elle poursuit en parlant du ton : "This tone is that of understatement, restraint, conciseness, and of biting, relentless humor" (2). D'autres critiques ont parlé d'autres éléments du style de Mavis Gallant. Je cite maintenant Neil Besner: "The promise of meaning in Gallant's stories is always an allusive spark, flashing out from tiny collisions of details, flickering quickly over nuances, lighting up a phrase, a state of mind, a landscape for a moment, and then subsiding into the steady glimmer of her fiction's surface and style" (*Light*,152). Je pourrais multiplier les citations et les commentaires sur le style mais on dit souvent que c'est en traduisant une oeuvre qu'on vient vraiment à la connaître; je donnerais donc la parole d'abord aux traducteurs, et ensuite aux critiques, pour un premier tour de table autour de la notion du style. Je dois dire que je suis très consciente—et j'en éprouve beaucoup de plaisir—de ce que Mavis Gallant soit ici avec nous. Cela ajoute beaucoup de profondeur à notre rencontre autour de son oeuvre. En même temps, c'est toujours un peu gênant, je crois; peut-être aussi gênant pour l'auteure, finalement, que pour les critiques, parce qu'on se trouve en face-à-face, sans la distance d'une écriture. Je crois que cela ajoutera beaucoup de chaleur à nos commentaires sur le style, et je vous remercie d'avance, Mavis Gallant, d'avoir accepté d'être des nôtres cet après-midi.

Alors Pierre-Edmond, comme vous êtes le seul homme de notre table ronde, je m'amuserai à vous donner la parole en premier, pour vous priver, peut-être, d'avoir le dernier mot! Comment voyez-vous, après votre expérience de traduction, le style de Mavis Gallant?

P-ER: C'est ça, vous m'envoyez au casse-pipe en espérant que je n'en reviendrai pas! Vous avez dit tout à l'heure que lorsqu'on traduisait une oeuvre, on la comprenait intimement, de l'intérieur, d'abord parce qu'on la lit et qu'on la relit. C'est ce que le critique Jean Rousset disait lorsqu'il définissait son lecteur idéal, ce lecteur qui, à force de soin et d'attention, reconnaît les reliefs du texte, ces reliefs qui en signalent les points d'articulation principaux. La traduction est un des exercices, certainement, qui permet la compréhension intime d'un texte; l'établissement du texte à partir des manuscrits est un exercice du même type. Ça permet évidemment d'entrer dans le discours de l'auteur, avec tout ce que cela peut avoir d'agréable, et en même temps de quelque peu aliénant, il faut le reconnaître. Mais j'ai quelques scrupules à parler de traduction, parce que je ne suis guère traducteur. J'ai traduit Mavis Gallant, mais pour des raisons tout à fait contingentes. C'est un petit peu tôt, d'un point de vue rhétorique, dans une présentation, pour en arriver tout de suite à la digression, mais enfin dans mon cas, c'était l'essentiel, parce que je lisais Mavis Gallant alors que j'enseignais aux États-Unis, et je la lisais dans le *New Yorker*, qu'on lisait à la maison. Tout ce qu'elle écrivait m'intéressait parce qu'elle parlait de Paris; c'était d'abord pour cette raison-là. On a parlé ce matin, les intervenants ont parlé de cette écriture de l'exil. J'étais moi-même en exil, donc cette image de Paris que je distinguais dans ses textes me parlait. Ce Paris où les pavés brillent sous la pluie comme les cirés des policiers (c'est dans un de ses textes), ce Paris en noir et blanc—ce sont les photos de Robert Doisneau ou les films de Clouzot—évidemment évoquait des choses personnelles, et en même temps, c'était écrit en anglais, avec cette distance dont on a parlé ce matin, cet autre regard éclairant. Bref, ce sont toutes sortes de raisons qui m'ont fait aimer ce texte, et c'est ensuite par une amie commune que j'ai rencontré Mavis Gallant, à un moment où elle souhaitait faire traduire ses textes. Alors je me suis trouvé embarqué dans cette aventure, disons, en raison de la situation. J'en garde un souvenir précieux. Mais tout ça pour vous dire que le débat sur la traduction, doit-il être proche de la langue-source ou s'agit-il d'une véritable écriture, enfin tout ce débat, que vous connaissez, puisque c'est celui des écoles de traductologie, c'est un peu moins mon problème. Moi j'ai voulu récrire en français un texte qui me touchait.

AW: Merci beaucoup, Pierre-Edmond. On reviendra un peu plus tard aux défis de la traduction. J'aimerais demander maintenant à Geneviève Doze, qui a traduit d'autres écrivaines canadiennes-anglaises, comme Alice Munro, et d'autres auteures anglaises, si elle aimerait nous parler soit du style, soit de la façon dont elle a été amenée à traduire l'oeuvre de Gallant.

GD: Bon, j'irai un peu dans le même sens que Pierre-Edmond Robert, parce que la traductologie, ce n'est pas mon truc non plus, et que j'ai un besoin d'empathie avec l'oeuvre. Je l'habite; heureusement que j'ai connu Mavis Gallant et que j'ai pu un peu entrer, pas dans sa peau, mais en tout cas, dans sa façon de penser, ce qui m'a aidé; et puis, j'ai essayé de vivre ses personnages. Mais dire que ça m'a permis de connaître l'oeuvre, ce serait outrecuidant, parce que chaque nouvelle est une nouvelle oeuvre, et j'ai l'impression que si elle a choisi la nouvelle, c'est parce qu'elle a une multiplicité d'intérêts et de visions du monde que seule la nouvelle lui permet de traduire, avec tout ce qu'elle ressent. Alors moi, j'ai été amenée un peu par hasard à traduire ses livres, mais ça été une expérience extrêmement enrichissante et intéressante.

AW: Merci Geneviève. Je vois qu'on a un peu peur d'aborder la question de la traduction en tant que telle, ou c'est peut-être ma déformation de traductologue. J'aimerais demander maintenant à Jane de parler: comment vous avez été amenée à vous lancer, Jane, à la recherche de la réception française des oeuvres de Mavis Gallant.

JK: Ce qui m'intéresse, enfin, au point de vue recherche, c'est la réception des traductions et surtout, les différences au niveau de la réception. Par exemple, parce que la réception française est différente de la réception canadienne. Pourquoi les Français s'intéressent-ils vraiment aux Canadiens? C'est une question intéressante, d'autant plus qu'il y a au Canada des traducteurs québécois. Donc, pourquoi, par exemple, les auteurs canadiens-anglais qui vivent au Canada sont-ils publiés et traduits ici en France—avec parfois beaucoup de succès ? Tandis qu'au Québec, on a tendance, je ne dirais pas à les négliger, mais ils sont quand même moins connus et beaucoup moins lus. Donc, c'est le point de départ de mes recherches. Le cas de Mavis Gallant est intéressant, justement parce que c'est un peu l'exception. Ce que j'ai pu constater à propos de certains auteurs, par exemple Jane Urquhart, Carol Shields, c'est qu'ici en France, on s'intéresse vraiment beaucoup à l'idée canadienne. On s'intéresse beaucoup à la littérature canadienne pour avoir un regard sur le Canada. Ça se voit dans la réception même, je dirais, dans le choix, parfois, des auteurs. Dernièrement, pour le festival *Les belles étrangères*, on a choisi certains auteurs et on a parlé d'eux selon leur origine géographique. Donc on parlait toujours de leurs régions. Ce que j'ai pu constater, justement, de la réception critique de Mavis Gallant, c'est qu'effectivement, on ne peut pas, étant donné le sujet de l'exil, regarder l'oeuvre sous cet aspect-là. C'est-à-dire, on ne peut pas chercher effectivement dans l'oeuvre une vision canadienne, ou enfin une vision du Canada. Donc je trouve que Mavis Gallant est un cas à part, un cas tout à fait exceptionnel.

AW: Peut-être qu'on pourrait dire que l'une des grandes qualités de l'oeuvre de Mavis Gallant, c'est justement de dépasser le cadre strictement national de l'interprétation, et de s'offrir donc à l'échelle de l'universel un questionnement sur les moeurs humaines. Je reviendrai néanmoins au style. Est-ce que ce serait là, pour vous aussi Nicole, une des caractéristiques du style de Mavis Gallant? Mais libre à vous de proposer une digression aussi.

NC: Il semble que ce soit très difficile de définir le style de Mavis Gallant. Si on pouvait dire quelque chose de son style, ça serait qu'il est justement incontournable;bien des gens ont essayé de le définir d'une façon ou d'une autre. Je n'ai traduit qu'une nouvelle de Mavis Gallant, "The Accident." Ce qui me frappait dans sa prose, justement, c'est qu'on a l'impression—et je crois qu'il faut l'avoir traduite pour sentir cela—qu'on est toujours vis-à-vis un précipice: on choisit un mot, on ne sait si le mot traduit bien l'idée de l'auteure, car il y a tant de couches de sens—d'ailleurs avec un mot français, bien entendu, on n'a plus toutes les résonances, toutes les connotations que le mot anglais pouvait avoir au départ, la sonorité, le rythme, *etc*. On perd cela au départ. Par ailleurs il y un hiatus qui se crée du point de vue purement sémantique, puisque qu'on a l'impression que l'auteure laisse une grande place au lecteur pour reconstruire le texte, ce qui pose un problème d'interprétation lorsqu'on traduit.

AW: Est-ce que c'est le moment de parler des défis de l'oeuvre, les défis pour le traducteur? Je pense que Geneviève, vous aurez peut-être quelque chose à ajouter, d'après votre expérience?

GD: Oui, enfin le grand problème pour le traducteur, c'est que c'est si bien écrit qu'on ne trouve pas la fissure qui permet au traducteur de s'introduire —enfin moi personnellement, j'avais beaucoup de mal à pénétrer la phrase pour la mettre en français. Le français, qui est soi-disant une langue si limpide, ne parvenait pas—enfin, je ne l'ai jamais senti aussi lourd—à traduire l'acuité de la pensée de Mavis, son côté incisif, et j'ai énormément peiné.

AW: Pierre-Edmond, vous qui connaissez bien Proust, est-ce que cette expérience de lecture vous a aidé à faire face aux défis de la traduction?

P-ER: Oui je vous disais tout à l'heure, peut-être l'habitude de ce travail, mais sans doute dans son aspect théorique plutôt que dans son aspect pratique. Enfin Proust aussi a fait de la traduction, comme vous le savez, sans connaître l'anglais, puisqu'il a traduit deux ouvrages de John Ruskin.

AW: C'est peut-être un avantage de moins connaître l'autre langue!

P-ER: Enfin il se faisait faire le mot-à-mot, et il a traduit Ruskin à partir de ce mot-à-mot. Quand on lui faisait des reproches sur sa traduction, il disait: «Je ne connais peut-être pas l'anglais, mais je connais John Ruskin». Je dirais peut-être un peu la même chose à propos de Mavis Gallant; mais c'est vrai que la traduction est une oeuvre critique, également. En fait, ce que j'avais envie de dire de l'oeuvre de Mavis, je l'ai dit en faisant les traductions—plutôt qu'en faisant une étude critique. L'habitude, oui, de l'établissement du texte, parce que lorsque vous passez d'un côté à l'autre, c'est-à-dire du manuscrit au texte imprimé, ou bien du texte anglais au texte français, il faut que, comme dans un bilan comptable, tout ce qui était dans la colonne de gauche se retrouve dans la colonne de droite. Mais pour y parvenir, on est obligé de bouleverser pas mal de choses parce que, effectivement, la phrase de Mavis rassemble des impressions diverses. On l'a dit ce matin, je crois, à propos de l'aspect sensoriel—je l'ai entendu—qu'elle emprunte à des domaines divers, également à des catégories de pensées diverses, et en utilisant des termes qui permettront ce que vous venez de dire, Nicole, à l'instant, les couches successives de sens. Je crois que ça a été dit à l'instant; le problème est qu'effectivement le traducteur va être obligé de choisir entre des termes qui seront tous par définition imparfaits, et c'est par toutes sortes d'artifices qu'il réussira à introduire l'élément manquant, qui ne peut pas figurer dans le mot français particulier qui a été choisi.

AW: Est-ce qu'on a associé Proust à une certaine habitude de lecture,une certaine façon de lire Proust? Pour Jane ou pour Nicole, est-ce qu'il y aurait d'autres rapprochements à faire? Nicole, vous avez une longue expérience de Jane Urquhart, une autre écrivaine canadienne. Soit par contraste, soit par ressemblance, verriez-vous des rapprochements possibles? Peut-être que vous aimeriez poursuivre l'idée avancée par Pierre-Edmond?

NC: Pour le moment je vois plus de contrastes, mais j'imagine qu'il faudrait étudier cette question. J'ai l'impression que l'écriture d'Urquhart est beaucoup plus romantique—je sais que «romantique» est un mot très très galvaudé et qu'il ne faudrait pas l'utiliser dans ce sens—mais, même si Urquhart connaît bien l'ironie, on dirait que chez elle l'ironie s'établit de façon totalement différente et, d'une certaine façon, est peut-être moins dominante dans tout le texte. L'ironie chez Urquhart se limiterait à certains aspects, puisque ses textes respirent toujours un certain romantisme qui me semble absent chez Mavis Gallant. Ce que j'allais dire aussi du style de Mavis Gallant, c'est qu'on a l'impression que Mavis Gallant travaille son style comme Flaubert. C'est un très grand défi que de traduire Mavis Gallant, ou même de l'interpréter d'une façon ou d'une autre parce que c'est tellement immense comme oeuvre qu'il faut beaucoup de critiques et de traducteurs pour rendre tous les versants de l'oeuvre.

AW: Oui, effectivement nous avons avec nous aujourd'hui seulement deux des traducteurs de Mavis Gallant. Il y a également Jean Lambert, Eric Diacon et Suzanne Mayoux. Donc, ça fait toute une équipe de traducteurs pour une seule écrivaine, et c'est déjà un hommage à la complexité et à l'ampleur de l'oeuvre de Mavis Gallant. Ce que je trouve intriguant—et je ne sais pas si vous, vous auriez une réponse à ça, Jane—c'est que tout en écrivant en anglais, Mavis Gallant habite Paris et met souvent en scène Paris. Pierre-Edmond y a fait allusion en disant que c'était justement cette caractéristique parisienne de l'oeuvre qui l'avait attiré alors qu'il était à son tour exilé aux États-Unis. Est-ce que ça présente une difficulté particulière, le fait qu'on lise des histoires sur la France en anglais comme si les personnages étaient situés quelque part en France mais habitaient au sein de la langue anglaise, alors qu'en traduction française, ces mêmes personnages naviguent en français, en France? J'arrive à l'idée qu'il y a quelque chose dans cette oeuvre qui serait peut-être intraduisible, à une représentation assez particulière de la différence.

JK: Ça, je ne sais pas, enfin, encore là, ça contribue vraiment, je dirais, à la spécificité de l'oeuvre de Gallant, dans la mesure où, effectivement, nous avons des histoires à propos de Paris, écrites, rédigées par une Canadienne en anglais à Paris, mais traduites par la suite en français. Alors ça fait quand même une autre variété d'exil, effectivement. La traduction est toujours, je dirais, une espèce d'exil, mais dans ce cas-là, ça fait quand même quelque chose de vraiment exceptionnel. Et encore là, c'est une question de regard. On parlait de Jane Urquhart tout à l'heure; elle a dit à propos de son succès ici en France, et là je cite: "The public is interested in [...]the force of the landscape in my work" (O'Donnel,22). Donc, je pense que le public français lit Jane Urquhart pour d'autres raisons. Ainsi, on ne peut pas aborder l'oeuvre de Gallant de la même façon. Alors c'est un avantage, dans une certaine mesure, parce que justement, comme Agnès l'a dit tout à l'heure, on ne peut pas critiquer l'oeuvre en tant que regard sur le Canada. Il faut vraiment étudier la valeur littéraire, en fait justement le style, et dans la réception, enfin, des articles que j'ai lus, c'est justement de cela qu'on parle, c'est-à-dire qu'on parle beaucoup de style. Malheureusement on ne parle pas du traducteur, de la traduction. On parle de la traduction comme s'il s'agissait vraiment de l'original, mais on signale vraiment la valeur littéraire, ce qui n'est pas nécessairement le cas pour tous les auteurs. Mais je crois qu'effectivement, du point de vue marché commercial, je ne sais pas à quel point, enfin, je ne sais pas si c'est vraiment un avantage, dans la mesure où, si on veut vraiment chercher un regard sur le Canada, ce n'est pas dans une histoire à propos de Paris qu'on va le trouver nécessairement. Par contre, il faut dire que c'est quand même un regard différent. Encore là, je vous cite Charles Poore, du *New York Times*: "The farther away from her native Canada she takes the people, the more indelibly Canadian they become in their streets and straits of exile" ("Books," 3). Alors là, c'est à savoir à quel point c'est toujours un regard différent.

AW: Alors ce serait peut-être une des dimensions courageuses de l'oeuvre de Mavis Gallant, le fait qu'elle vient sur le terrain français tout en écrivant en anglais, et qu'elle propose un regard plus intime sur la société française tout en épousant le regard de l'exilé. Là, je vous vois réagir, Geneviève. J'essaie de piquer au vif les sensibilités, alors peut-être que j'aurai réussi.

GD: Non, moi je vois plutôt un regard d'ethnologue, parce qu'elle fait ressortir des choses qu'enfin, moi je ne vois pas, ou que j'essaie de ne pas voir. Elle les taille au scalpel et je pense que les écrivains français probablement ne le feraient pas.

AW: Est-ce qu'on pourrait vous demander des exemples? Est-ce que cet aspect-là, au fur et à mesure que vous traduisiez l'oeuvre, vous est apparu, une fois revenu à Paris, Pierre-Edmond? Est-ce que *Rue de Lille*, que vous avez lu avec peut-être un brin de nostalgie à l'égard de la France, une fois de retour —étiez-vous toujours aux États-Unis au moment où vous avez traduit l'oeuvre?

P-ER: Non j'étais de retour en France quand j'ai fait cette traduction. Oui, effectivement, le regard a changé. D'une part, comme je disais tout à l'heure, la traduction impose des relectures nombreuses, permet d'approfondir la connaissance du texte, mais je crois que la question que vous posiez portait sur, au fond, le contenu; on pourrait dire le contenu sociologique des nouvelles, non? C'était dans ce sens que vous le vouliez?

AW: Moi je ne veux rien, je pose la question.

P-ER: Voilà; je vais continuer par rapport à ce qui avait été dit. Le fait que Mavis Gallant a abordé la réalité française d'une manière différente de celle d'écrivains, de romanciers, de nouvellistes contemporains—oui mais c'est le privilège du regard extérieur, ça; c'est le privilège de quelqu'un qui connaît intimement la réalité française, tout en utilisant un système de référence extérieur à cette réalité. C'est de ce contact entre les deux, entre un outil et cette réalité que naît ce décalage à la fois attachant et si riche des oeuvres de Mavis. Je voulais ajouter que c'est une tradition, d'ailleurs, qui existe depuis les années vingt au moins, ces écrivains de langue anglaise vivant à Paris et parlant la réalité française. Mais habituellement, ils ne vivaient que dans leur milieu d'expatriés; ici c'est la réalité la plus française qui figure. Il suffit de comparer pour s'en rendre compte. Quelquefois avec Mavis nous commentons les articles que nous lisons dans le journal américain de Paris, le *Herald Tribune*, et on se dit: comment est-ce Dieu possible? Voilà des gens qui vivent à Paris depuis tant d'années et ils n'ont rien compris, ils continuent à reproduire des clichés sans se rendre compte que la réalité est autrement complexe. Alors ici vous avez effectivement, en dehors de toutes les autres qualités dont nous parlons, un témoignage authentique.

AW: Est-ce que je peux demander à Geneviève et à Pierre-Edmond de nous parler un petit peu du processus de la traduction? Est-ce que vous avez eu l'occasion—puisque là c'est un défi pour vous—vous traduisez un auteur, ou une auteure, comme on dirait au Québec, qui maîtrise le français, donc qui serait susceptible de porter un regard assez perspicace sur la traduction en tant que telle. Pourriez-vous nous parler un peu du processus éditorial et à la fois des contacts que vous avez eus avec Mavis Gallant au cours de la traduction? Comment ça s'est passé?

GD: Oh, j'ai eu l'occasion de l'interroger plusieurs fois sur des termes que je ne connaissais pas parce qu'il y en a certains qui sont proprement canadiens. Par la suite, Mavis a relu la traduction et a fait des annotations qui nécessitaient une relecture de ma part et des corrections. Une collaboration.

AW: C'est toujours, comment dirais-je, c'est toujours une gageure quand on donne son texte à l'auteur et qu'on veut bien faire; en même temps, la transposition dans une autre langue est chose complexe et nuancée. Dans votre cas, Pierre-Edmond, est-ce qu'il y a eu aussi un dialogue avec l'auteure?

P-ER: C'était même un dialogue à plusieurs voix pour le premier parce qu'il y avait beaucoup de cuisiniers, comme on dirait en anglais. C'est-à-dire–

AW: C'est-à-dire-beaucoup de cuisiniers au lieu d'avoir un seul chef, quoi.

P-ER: Non, non, non. Ce n'est pas ce que je voulais dire, mais la petite maison d'édition—parce qu'avant d'être repris dans la collection 10/18 (c'est l'édition que vous avez là), *Rue de Lille* avait d'abord été publié par une petite maison d'édition. Alors il y avait deux personnes, plus la secrétaire-réceptionniste, *etc.*, qui donnait son avis (rires). C'était tout à fait sympathique, d'ailleurs. Moi, comme je ne me voyais pas en traducteur professionnel, je n'étais pas du tout vexé. Par exemple, cette jeune femme sans doute devait trouver que j'étais un vieux monsieur parce que j'employais des expressions qui à son avis ne s'employaient pas chez les moins de 25 ans. Elle m'en avait fait la remarque deux ou trois fois. Bon, dans un deuxième temps, Mavis m'a fait des propositions sur un certain nombre de choses et je crois qu'on s'est très bien entendus là-dessus. Mais ce n'est pas gênant, d'ailleurs, qu'il y ait plusieurs personnes qui interviennent; je crois que c'est plutôt bien; on n'est pas obligé de suivre les conseils de tout un chacun, mais quelquefois ça vous oblige à repenser à vos propres choix, à les justifier.

AW: Est-ce que pour vous, Geneviève, il y a eu une intervention semblable de la part de l'éditeur?

GD: Ah oui. Oui bien sûr, mais j'en étais très reconnaissante parce que ça oblige à repenser à ce qu'on a fait et qu'on n'a jamais assez de recul. On a beau se relire, on ne voit pas l'oeuvre assez calmement pour éviter les erreurs et, encore une fois, comme je disais tout à l'heure, les lourdeurs. C'était dans le sens de la légèreté qu'il fallait travailler, quitte à couper des phrases là où elles n'étaient pas coupées dans le texte, et des paragraphes aussi, à les fragmenter.

AW: Là vous abordez un autre sujet, qui concerne la transposition d'une oeuvre d'une langue à l'autre et chaque langue a son génie, comme on aime dire. Est-ce qu'on a parlé de la virtuosité stylistique de Mavis Gallant? Est-ce que le français—je pose une question que seule peut-être une Canadienne anglaise pourrait poser, est-ce que le français a été à la hauteur du style de Mavis Gallant? Est-ce que tout ce que véhiculait ce style finement façonné en anglais pouvait se transposer en français? Est-ce que c'était compatible avec le génie? Je pense aux structures des verbes, aux verbes modaux. Est-ce qu'il y avait des aspects qui posaient plus de difficultés pour le traducteur? Je ne sais pas si Nicole, vous auriez…

NC: Je n'ai traduit qu'une nouvelle de Mavis Gallant, alors mon expérience est très limitée. C'est très gênant de parler de génie de la langue parce que surtout à notre époque, on a l'impression que les langues n'ont plus de frontières aussi étanches; cela dit, on a affaire à deux langues bien différentes, quoiqu'elles aient des territoires communs, de par leurs traditions.

AW: Et vous avez parlé tantôt d'ambiguïté, qu'en traduisant il fallait quand même se résoudre à ce que la même ambiguïté ne soit pas toujours possible en français. Enfin ce n'est pas un jugement de valeur, c'est tout simplement qu'on a affaire à deux langues qui fonctionnent différemment, et qu'ici la langue d'origine est bien exploitée par le texte original. Il faut parfois trouver une compensation.

NC: Oui, tout à fait. Moi j'ai eu de la difficulté parce que j'essayais de traduire plus fidèlement le style de Mme Gallant. Il fallait respecter les caractéristiques stylistiques du français, tout en respectant le style de Mme Gallant. Et là, on tombe de Charybde en Scylla parce que tout en étant fidèle à l'un, par exemple à l'auteure, on renie un petit peu la langue française, qui a ses traditions, qui a des racines différentes. Par ailleurs, je dirais qu'on est sur un terrain très glissant, c'est-à-dire que, autant la prose de Mavis Gallant est solide, autant elle est sujette à interprétation, comme tout le monde l'a bien vu. Nécessairement, il faut prendre position quand on traduit, et cela pose un problème d'ordre éthique. C'est-à-dire qu'il faut choisir une interprétation: on ne peut pas laisser toutes les connotations, toute les virtualités de l'anglais parce que c'est la langue de Mavis Gallant qui est à l'oeuvre. Il y a peut-être un petit noyau dénotatif, mais tout le reste, si vous voulez, c'est comme quand on lance un caillou dans un lac. De nombreux cercles se créent autour de l'endroit où la pierre est tombée. De la même façon, Gallant jette un mot monosyllabique, et de nombreuses ondes connotatives se créent, qui sont dans la tradition anglo-saxonne, donc qui travaillent tout à fait dans le grain de la langue anglaise, et en même temps qui appartiennent à l'univers de Mavis Gallant.

AW: Pierre-Edmond, je vois que vous avez l'air d'être d'accord avec Nicole.

P-ER: Oui j'étais tout à fait d'accord avec cette analyse qui soulignait les difficultés évidemment que le traducteur ne peut manquer de rencontrer. Mais il faut que le résultat soit du français, qu'on retrouve le ton, si particulier de l'auteur, la musique, et que le rythme—même si celui du français n'a rien à voir avec celui de l'anglais—que le rythme évoque quand même quelque chose qui existait dans la langue d'origine. Alors est-ce qu'on réussit ce tour de force chaque fois? Non, mais il mérite d'être tenté. Il vaut mieux quelquefois s'écarter un peu afin de pouvoir conserver ce ton, conserver ce rythme, et donner au moins l'impression de cette multiplicité de sens, même quand on ne peut pas toujours tous les glisser dans la phrase.

GD: Je voudrais ajouter que chaque fois que ça a été possible, j'ai essayé de traduire d'une traite une nouvelle parce que dans chacune l'atmosphère est parfaitement cohérente, et que quand on traduit en plusieurs fois, on ne peut pas établir cette unité; il y en a certaines qui étaient beaucoup trop longues pour pouvoir le faire, mais enfin, c'était une tentative.

AW: J'aimerais maintenant ouvrir le débat et inviter l'assistance à poser des questions aux participants et aux participantes de la table ronde. Je vois que Danielle Schaub a déjà levé la main.

D Schaub: Une des choses qui m'intéresse très fort—bon, moi je n'ai jamais lu l'oeuvre de Mavis Gallant qu'en anglais—mais quand je lis, je me dis:

comment, mais comment est-ce que les traducteurs peuvent traduire certaines tournures de phrases? Et je pense en particulier aux changements de temps, aux verbes modaux, qui sont en anglais très riches, qui sont des colles pour nous critiques, parce qu'il nous est déjà arrivé de discuter de l'utilisation de verbes modaux, et de nous dire: oui mais là, il y a cette nuance-là, où l'on voit vraiment différents niveaux. Comment faites-vous dans la traduction pour rendre ça? Est-ce que vous ressentez la même complexité que je sens? Évidemment, je suis mal placée maintenant: j'aurais dû lire vos traductions, mais est-ce que ce n'est pas un problème quand vous traduisez les nouvelles?

GD: Oui c'est évidemment un problème; quand je parlais tout à l'heure de lourdeur, c'est ce que je voulais dire, parce que nous sommes obligés de faire des périphrases et d'ajouter des choses pour rendre ces modalités.

AW: Est-ce qu'on peut proposer un petit quelque chose que je n'ai pas pensé proposer aux panélistes avant—je leur avais envoyé quand même quelques mots avec des questions—alors là, je quitte l'ordre du jour prévu—mais est-ce qu'on pourrait vous proposer la lecture d'un petit paragraphe de l'original d'une nouvelle, suivi d'une lecture du même paragraphe en français? J'ai avec moi justement de «De l'autre côté du pont», qui est la traduction de "Across the Bridge"—oui, j'ai toujours envie de dire "Crossing the Bridge." Je sais bien qu'il y a toute une distinction d'ailleurs—, de Geneviève Doze. J'ai aussi *Rue de Lille*, dont la traduction a été faite par Pierre-Edmond Robert. Il me faut un lecteur, une lectrice anglophone, peut-être Linda, est-ce que vous liriez l'original? On va essayer de trouver pendant qu'on cherche "Across the Bridge" (La nouvelle éponyme). Je l'ai ici, donc on pourrait commencer par la traduction de Geneviève Doze.

L Leith: C'est le premier paragraphe de "Across the Bridge": "We were walking over the bridge from the Place de la Concorde, my mother and I—arm in arm, like two sisters who never quarrel. She had the invitations to my wedding in a leather shopping bag: I was supposed to be getting married to Arnaud Pons. My father's first cousin, Gaston Castelli, deputy for a district in the South, had agreed to frank the envelopes. He was expecting us at the Palais Bourbon, at the other end of the bridge. His small office looked out on nothing of interest, just a wall and some windows. A typist who did not seem to work for anyone in particular sat outside his door. He believed she was there to spy on him, and for that reason had told my mother to keep the invitations out of sight" (*Selected Stories*,118).

GD: Lecture du premier paragraphe de «De l'autre côté du pont»: «Nous traversions à pied le pont de la Concorde, ma mère et moi, bras dessus bras dessous, comme deux soeurs qui ne se disputent jamais. Elle portait mes faire-part de mariage dans un cabas en cuir: j'allais épouser Arnaud Pons, et Gaston Castelli, cousin germain de mon père, député d'une circonscription du Midi, avait accepté d'affranchir ce courrier. Il nous attendait au Palais Bourbon, de l'autre côté du pont. Son petit bureau ne donnait sur rien d'intéressant, seulement un mur et quelques fenêtres. Une dactylo qui ne paraissait pas avoir d'attribution précise était installée devant sa porte; il pensait qu'elle était là pour l'espionner, et c'est pour cette raison qu'il avait demandé à ma mère de cacher les enveloppes» (*De l'autre côté du pont*, p. 99). Alors je peux déjà commenter que le «j'allais épouser» évidemment réduit l'original.

AW: Alors on passera à «Rue de Lille», c'est la nouvelle éponyme du recueil traduit par Pierre-Edmond.

L Leith: Lecture du premier paragraphe de «Rue de Lille» en anglais: "My second wife, Juliette, died in the apartment on rue de Lille, where she had lived—at first alone, more or less, then with me—since the end of the war. All the rooms gave on to the ivy-hung well of a court, and were for that reason dark. We often talked about looking for a brighter flat, on a top floor with southern exposure and a wide terrace, but Parisians seldom move unless they're driven to. 'We know the worst of what we've got, we told each other. It's better than a bad surprise' " (*Selected Stories*, 817).

P-ER: Oui, ce premier paragraphe nous avait posé un certain nombre de problèmes, en particulier la deuxième phrase. Je me rappelle d'une conversation avec votre agent Michelle Lapautre, anglophone, mais qui n'avait pas compris la totalité de cette phrase en anglais, alors—vous vous rappelez? —Oui, et ce premier paragraphe est d'une telle richesse que pour passer en français, les phrases débordaient: «Ma seconde femme, Juliette, est morte dans l'appartement de la rue de Lille, là où elle avait vécu—d'abord seule, plus ou moins, ensuite avec moi—depuis la fin de la guerre. Toutes les pièces donnaient sur une cour, un puits drapé de lierre, et pour cette raison, elles étaient sombres. Nous avons souvent envisagé en paroles de chercher un logement plus clair, un dernier étage exposé au midi avec une vaste terrasse, mais les Parisiens ne finissent par déménager que lorsqu'ils y sont forcés. "Nous savons ce qu'il y a de pire dans ce que nous avons," nous disions-nous. "Cela vaut mieux qu'une mauvaise surprise"» (*Rue de Lille*, p. 5).

AW: Alors ça vous a peut-être donné de quoi savourer à la fois Mavis Gallant en anglais et en français. Je ne sais pas, Mme Gallant, si vous avez envie de nous dire aussi quelque chose ? Peut-être plus tard ?

P Sabor: Moi j'ai une petite question au sujet de "My Second Wife," qui est devenu «Ma seconde femme». Comment avez-vous trouvé *seconde,* plutôt que *deuxième*?

P-ER: Il y a une règle en français: *seconde*, c'est lorsqu'il n'y en a que deux, et *deuxième,* ça implique qu'il y en a une troisième (*rires*).

P Sabor: Je pose la question parce que ce sont des choses qu'on dit aux lecteurs français qui ne sont pas dites en anglais.

P-ER: Oui, vous avez parfaitement raison. On dit quelque chose aux lecteurs français qu'on ne dit pas en anglais.

P Sabor: Ça m'a frappé qu'en anglais, la formulation est ambiguë, alors que le français, lui, est très précis.

AW: Est-ce qu'il y aurait d'autres questions à poser aux panélistes? Je ne sais pas si vous avez été sensibles à ce phénomène, mais les traducteurs, en général, ont une énorme générosité à l'égard de l'oeuvre qu'ils traduisent, mais aiment rester un petit peu invisibles. C'est toujours difficile de les amener à parler du processus concret. Cependant chacun est intervenu tout de suite pour dire quelque chose qui montre qu'ils ont beaucoup réfléchi à leur travail. Geneviève, pour dire: «Ah oui! J'aurais pu faire autre chose pour la traduction de "I was supposed to marry Arnaud Pons"»; et avant de lire, Pierre-Edmond a aussi parlé un peu de la difficulté de la traduction. Alors je crois qu'on sent tout de suite dans cette réaction très spontanée tout le défi que présente la traduction, et peut-être en particulier la traduction d'une oeuvre aussi serrée, aussi complexe que celle de Mavis Gallant.

JK: J'allais dire tout simplement que ce qu'on voit dans la réception critique, c'est justement, comme j'ai dit tout à l'heure, l'aspect littéraire, la valeur littéraire; donc je trouve que nous avons vraiment à féliciter les traducteurs pour avoir rendu cette valeur littéraire, cet aspect. On parle justement de l'art du non-dit, par exemple à propos de «De l'autre côté du pont». Donc vous avez su rendre, enfin, ne pas trop interpréter, rendre les vides, et c'est la même chose à propos de «Rue de Lille». Je pense qu'effectivement, c'est très important de signaler le succès de ces traductions de ce point de vue-là.

AW: Il y a un terme que j'ai essayé d'éviter, en lisant un peu sur Mavis Gallant, et en particulier sur les entrevues qu'elle a accordées: c'est l'aspect canadien de son oeuvre. C'est peut-être dans le but de ne pas la camper comme écrivaine canadienne, pour lui laisser la liberté d'être tout simplement écrivaine. Mais il est certain que quand on regarde un peu la réception de l'oeuvre de Gallant—et Jane, vous avez cité un passage d'un critique américain qui parlait de cet aspect canadien—je ne sais pas si les traducteurs, si Geneviève ou Pierre-Edmond, vous avez été sensibles à ce regard extérieur sur la France ? Est-ce qu'il y a là quelque chose dans l'extériorité de ce regard qui vous a frappé? Je pense, Geneviève, aux traductions que vous faites d'Alice Munro. On a beaucoup parlé de défi; il y a dans la salle Jacques Leclaire, directeur du Centre International au Centre d'études canadiennes à Rouen, qui trouve que souvent en littérature canadienne, tant du côté anglophone que du côté francophone, il y a une notion de défi. Je ne sais pas s'il y aurait là un terrain, quelques pistes de réflexion, tout en laissant à Mme Gallant son statut d'écrivaine sans qualificatifs. Est-ce qu'il y aurait là quelque chose, des pistes de réflexion par rapport à Alice Munro, par exemple?

GD: Je ne sais que dire. Je pense qu'il y a, comment dire, une certaine cruauté qui me frappe, parce qu'*a priori*, ce n'est pas une littérature dont on attendrait une dureté. Aussi un intérêt pour la société, pour tous les niveaux de la société; des relations sociales, peut-être plus présentes que dans la littérature française, par exemple.

J Leclaire: L'idée que j'essayais de faire ressortir, c'est que cette notion de défi était souvent ce besoin d'imposer un plan personnel à la contingence. Bien sûr, on peut dire qu'on va le trouver finalement dans tout roman, dans tout texte. On peut dire aussi qu'on le trouve en littérature américaine. Ce qui m'a frappé, je me trompe peut-être, mais c'est que dans la littérature canadienne, ce défi est en quelque sorte valorisé en tant que tel, sans forcément considérer une issue favorable plutôt que défavorable. C'est-à-dire le fait de mener cette lutte contre tout ce qui peut s'opposer à vous est en soi valorisé. Alors il me semble qu'assez souvent on peut reconnaître une touche canadienne, en étant très prudent, comme on retrouve une touche américaine chez Hemingway quand il vous parle du Kilimandjaro. C'est-à-dire qu'il y a une approche qui me semble intéressante. J'avais été frappé, quand j'écoutais la télévision canadienne ou québécoise, du fait que les mots *challenge*, *défi* revenaient en permanence. Il ne se passait pas une émission sans que je les entende. Et je me disais qu'après tout, même si on se réfère à quelqu'un d'aussi ancien que Taine, finalement les Canadiens sont quand même face à un espace, à une histoire qui sont un défi permanent. Donc, d'une façon ou d'une autre, il ne serait pas étonnant de retrouver cela en littérature. Voilà en gros quelle était mon idée en toute modestie. Il y a une dernière question que j'aimerais poser à Mavis Gallant. J'avais entendu dire à *Village Voice* une chose qui m'avait beaucoup impressionné. Quand vous cherchiez à évaluer la qualité d'une traduction, vous aimiez beaucoup lire d'une part alternativement la traduction et le texte original, sans lire forcément les mêmes paragraphes, pour voir si c'était bien toujours la même voix que vous entendiez.

MG: Ça, c'est l'oeuvre de quelqu'un d'autre. Ça n'a rien à voir avec moi. Je sais que vous parlez du roman de Margaret Atwood et j'avais lu la traduction avec l'anglais mais pas les mêmes passages, non, non. Je continuais à lire en français; après je reprenais où je l'avais laissé en anglais et j'ai vu que vraiment ça coulait merveilleusement. Donc, pour moi, c'était une bonne traduction. Ce n'est pas spécialement en lisant les mêmes choses, parce que l'anglais et le français n'ont rien en commun, ni les mêmes mots ni la même résonance, pas du tout, pas seulement linguistiquement, mais historiquement. Là je mettrais une heure à vous expliquer ce que je veux dire, mais l'histoire de chaque mot, de la racine au temps présent, est différente, est entendue différemment et utilisée d'une autre façon. Je ne sais pas si vous pouvez comprendre.

J Leclaire: Ça souligne encore la difficulté des traductions.

MG: Ah, bien ça, je n'en doute pas.

AW: Alors quelques pistes: la cruauté peut-être chez les écrivains canadiens, le défi. Je pense qu'il faut sortir des éléments nouveaux sans autocensure. La question du défi possible, et puis là, un autre élément évoqué par Mavis Gallant, c'est cette séparation entre l'anglais et le français. Les mots, même ceux qui auraient les mêmes racines, subiraient une séparation historique, donc connaîtraient une histoire différente et auraient donc des résonances différentes. C'est ce qui explique peut-être l'hésitation de Geneviève Doze face à une phrase comme "I was supposed to marry Arnaud Pons" et sa traduction «Je devais épouser», formulation qui semble plutôt probable, ou enfin qui est ambiguë d'une autre manière, ce que vous auriez voulu éviter?

GD: Je ne me rappelle plus pourquoi j'ai choisi cette manière, mais je pense que c'était par économie. Pour ne pas faire une phrase trop contournée.

AW: C'est là où il y a quand même une série de pertes et de gains, dans la mesure où quelques nuances résistent à la traduction?

GD: Oui, de toute façon, on est toujours obligé de faire des sacrifices dans l'intérêt du rythme, de la phrase. Il faut jeter quelque chose à la mer.

AW: Alors je reviens à la question de cette dimension canadienne ou à la difficulté de la traduction. Je vois que Pierre-Edmond, vous réfléchissez. Auriez-vous aussi peut-être un autre substantif? Défi? cruauté?

P-ER: *Cruauté*, ça fait noir. *Défi* je n'en suis pas sûr, mais je ne connais pas suffisamment la littérature canadienne pour oser autre chose qu'une comparaison avec le whisky national *Canadian Club*, qui effectivement est à mi-chemin de ses parents anglais et américain—mais ça c'est pour plaisanter. En réalité je voudrais—et alors peut-être est-ce que pour les spécialistes ici de la littérature canadienne, ça aura un sens—revenir sur la conception de l'écrivain et la définition de la nouvelle, si je peux prendre une minute là-dessus. De l'écrivain raconteur d'histoires, comme le disait Anthony Burgess, par opposition au romancier qui, en France, est censé être en même temps une sorte de maître à penser—enfin il n'y parvient que bien rarement, mais il y a toujours cette prétention en tout cas, et la réception va dans ce sens. Et ici nous avons d'abord des histoires, alors qu'il y a bien d'autres choses certainement, mais nous avons d'abord des histoires. Il est possible que la littérature française ait perdu ce goût pour les histoires, ait perdu confiance dans les pouvoirs de la *mimesis*. Je pensais à ça en lisant un texte qui date du XVIIe siècle et que vous connaissez peut-être. C'est l'histoire du Maréchal de Bassompierre et de la belle lingère. C'est un texte court, une nouvelle à la Mavis Gallant en réalité, qui se trouve inséré dans les mémoires du Maréchal de Bassompierre. C'est une histoire assez curieuse. Le Maréchal a l'habitude de passer par le petit pont—nous connaissons tous ce coin de Paris—et là, dans une des boutiques, il y a une lingère qui lui fait toujours des sourires extraordinaires. Le Maréchal de Bassompierre est bel homme; il a l'habitude que les femmes se jettent à son cou, alors finalement il demande à son valet d'arranger un rendez-vous. Il y en aura un premier et puis un deuxième, mais le deuxième terminera court: il découvrira dans le lieu de rendez-vous des cadavres et on ne saura jamais de qui il s'agit. L'histoire s'arrête. Le Maréchal de Bassompierre doit repartir en mission le lendemain et il nous raconte ses souvenirs, et c'est à nous de tirer la morale de l'histoire. Que s'est-t-il passé? Est-ce que c'est une tentative pour le déconsidérer? Est-ce qu'on a cherché à dérober sa bourse en l'attirant par le biais de cette femme? Est-ce qu'elle était sincèrement éprise de lui? On ne le saura jamais. Eh bien, ce genre d'histoire est rare aujourd'hui dans la littérature française, parce qu'on a introduit d'autres ambitions, qui nous ont détournés de ce regard sur la réalité. Et lorsque je lisais Mavis, j'étais toujours sensible à ça, c'est-à-dire que nous avions à la fois le regard, le défilé des choses et la reconstruction.

AW: Et à la fin, le défi pour le lecteur, enfin l'ambivalence, l'ambiguïté plutôt, de l'histoire. En fait vous évoquez là quelque chose d'intéressant aussi dans la tradition de ce qu'on appellerait en anglais la *short story*. La tradition américaine et anglaise de la *short story* est très différente, finalement, par rapport à la tradition française de la nouvelle, et souvent d'ailleurs, la nouvelle en français est un genre un peu problématique, par rapport à la réception, certainement au XXe siècle. Nicole, est-ce que vous auriez quelques éléments à ajouter à ce sujet, parce que ça intervient certainement au niveau de la traduction, aussi au niveau de la réception des nouvelles de Mavis Gallant?

NC: Je pensais à la nouvelle québécoise, qui est souvent une nouvelle de l'obsession, et où il y a encore souvent une chute, un peu comme il y en avait par exemple en France au XIXe siècle avec Maupassant. Alors qu'avec Mavis Gallant, évidemment il n'y a pas de chute; et l'ambiguïté est présente dans toute l'histoire. C'est tout à fait vrai que dans la nouvelle canadienne-anglaise—c'est très particulier—il y a cette tradition narrative, c'est-à-dire que la narration elle-même est présentée comme intéressante. Ce n'est pas seulement un exercice de style. Chez Mavis Gallant, il me semble, il y a un style extraordinaire, qui à la fois participe de la définition de la nouvelle—brève, concise, dense—et à la fois conserve la narration d'une histoire, qui est quelque chose de très thérapeutique, parce qu'il y a processus, des humains en voie de changement. Mais en même temps, ce qui me semble particulier à l'univers de Gallant, c'est que dans toutes ses nouvelles, il y a non seulement l'histoire, mais en même temps tout un miroitement. Je ne sais même pas comment expliquer cela; c'est un miroitement du language,qui renvoie à différente réalités, évoquées, plutôt qu'explicitement décrites. C'est comme si chaque petite histoire était un prisme qui reflétait d'autres réalités.

Ici (loin du micro) discussion entre Marta Dvorak et Danielle Schaub à savoir si les nouvelles de Gallant tiennent plus de l'impressionisme ou du cubisme.

NC: Le jeu avec la lumière des Impressionnistes aussi. À la fois forme et lumière, qui est couleur aussi. J'ai l'impression que vous avez toutes les deux raison, que ça joue sur tous ces plans à la fois.

D Schaub: En fait les deux réalités fonctionnent très bien, et comme l'expliquait Marta, finalement entre un groupe et l'autre, il n'y avait en fait pas une barrière très précise; c'est vrai que le côté impressionniste y était, mais le côté cubiste aussi; c'est une combinaison des deux, et c'est ce qui en fait la richesse.

AW: Est-ce qu'il y aurait d'autres questions de la salle? Peut-être qu'on pourrait demander à Madame Gallant si elle aimerait dire un mot maintenant, non pas pour clôturer le débat, mais pour nous donner encore un défi?

MG: Je n'ai rien à dire pour moi-même, mais si vous avez une question, je répondrai volontiers.

AW: Alors merci.

NC: Tout à l'heure vous avez parlé des différences entre les deux langues. Vous en parlez souvent—par exemple dans l'introduction de *Home Truths*, je crois que vous avez parlé de ces différences entre l'anglais et le français. Je me souviens plus mais je l'ai vu quelque part.

MG: Moi non plus, écoutez ça fait quinze ans que j'ai écrit cela et je n'ai jamais relu, alors si vous pouvez me dire ce que j'ai dit (*rires*).

NC: J'ai une mémoire impressionniste—et là, ce n'est pas une qualité—et ce que j'allais vous demander, c'est: tout à l'heure, vous avez dit que vous pourriez parler pendant des heures des différences entre l'anglais et le français, et ça me fascine parce que j'ai eu l'impression que vous touchiez à quelque chose que les gens aujourd'hui ne veulent plus aborder, c'est-à-dire à ces différences, comme vous avez dit, extrêmement précises entre l'anglais et le français.

MG: Ce sont les langues que je connais le mieux. Ce sont les seules que je comprenne bien. On n'a pas en anglais ou en français la même conversation. On ne parle pas du même sujet. On ne peut pas. Le plus difficile, c'est d'avoir des conversations bilingues où on est peut-être la seule qui comprenne et qui puisse dire: mais il a dit ceci, non mais ce n'est pas cela exactement. Ou: on ne dirait pas la même chose de la même façon en anglais. Ça serait, vous comprenez, ce n'est pas simplement la traduction d'une chose à l'autre. C'est le sujet même. Là, je ne vous parle pas de l'écriture, je vous parle de la conversation comme cela. On ne dit pas les mêmes choses.

NC: Dans *Home Truths*, vous aviez dit quelque chose comme, à chaque fois qu'un anglophone parle—peut-être que je vous interprète—il a envie de raconter une petite anecdote, alors que le francophone, le Français par exemple, va commenter. Est-ce que je me trompe?

MG: Il y aurait une suite abstraite, ce qui en anglais est intolérable. Non mais c'est vrai, on souffre, si c'est en anglais. Je parle de conversation, mais l'abstraction est adaptée au français et le français est adapté à sa norme, qui prête à l'abstraction. (*À* Pierre-Edmond Robert) Est-ce que vous êtes d'accord? Bon. Vous auriez dit non, j'aurais pleuré.

JK: Tout simplement donc, enfin, regardez Nicole, je ne sais pas si ce serait: "The French taste for abstraction sails close to rhetoric and can sound false or insincere to an English-speaking listener, while a conversation in English, with its succession of illustrative anecdotes that take their departure from a point, rather than lead to one, soon bores a mind trained in French" ("Introduction," *Home Truths*, xviii).

MG: Mais je crois que oui. Je l'écrirais encore aujourd'hui. Je crois que c'est cela.

AW: Est-ce que je peux me permettre de vous poser une question? Si en fait on ne parle pas de la même chose en anglais et en français, quand vous écrivez en anglais et que vous mettez en scène des personnages français qui sont en train de converser, comment vous tirez-vous d'affaires?

MG: Mais je fais plus attention, c'est tout. C'est exactement comme lorsque j'écris du point de vue d'un homme et c'est *je*, *moi*, mais c'est un homme. Je fais très très attention. Ce n'est pas la même chose. Les émotions n'ont pas la même source. C'est autre chose. Je fais vraiment [attention], quand je relis une nouvelle qui est située en France et que tous les personnages sont Français, ou ils sont Français entre eux, il n'y a pas d'observation extérieure, parce que je ne le fais presque plus maintenant. Je le relis en me disant, est-ce qu'il ferait ça? Est-ce qu'il pense ça? Est-ce que sa jalousie serait comme cela? Est-ce qu'elle chercherait par tous les moyens à savoir qui est l'autre femme ou non? C'est très différent. Il faut tout simplement être attentif à ce qu'on fait. On ne peut pas prendre quelqu'un d'anglophone, changer son nom et en faire un francophone. Ce n'est pas possible. C'est comme prendre quelqu'un qui est peintre et qui parle, et dire: bon je vais le décrire comme écrivain, ça marchera: ça ne marche pas. Il faut faire très attention, à tout. Je ne sais pas si c'est clair.

AW: C'est très clair et on a déjà le sens du détail qui caractérise votre style, un souci d'authencité dans le détail.

MG: Je sais que quand j'ai commencé à situer une fiction à Paris, au départ, il y a très très longtemps—c'était en 1951—les Français sont observés et vus et incompris par une Américaine. Même là, ça ne faisait pas longtemps que j'étais là, mais je comprenais qu'elle ne comprenait pas, qu'il y avait un mystère que moi-même je n'avais pas élucidé. Donc je l'ai laissé comme cela. Par la suite j'ai écrit de plus en plus, il y avait tout le temps un observateur, une observatrice, qui était généralement de langue anglaise; ça pouvait être autre chose, mais pas le français. Après il y avait—et ça, je l'ai remarqué quand je ramassais les nouvelles pour ce gros livre que j'ai vu quelque part, oui, et je les relisais et je voyais—il est arrivé un stade où ça faisait vingt ans que j'étais en France, et c'étaient des Français qui observaient des étrangers: je me mettais inconsciemment à leur place, et après, c'étaient des Français entre eux. Ça, c'était *Rue de Lille*: ce sont des Français entre eux, pour la plupart, et ça venait tout naturellement, je n'ai pas forcé.

AW: Quand vous avez relu votre préface à ce choix de nouvelles, en vous relisant, est-ce que vous avez eu d'autres observations sur votre—je n'ose pas dire «évolution», mais—sur les changements au fil des années, au fil des nouvelles?

MG: Vous parlez de la nouvelle même?

AW: Peut-être pas. Des sujets, vous avez évoqué des changements de perspective.

MG: C'est ça, j'avais remarqué en le faisant.

AW: Et pour les nouvelles canadiennes situées au Canada, est-ce que vous aviez eu—?

MG: Mémoire, mémoire. C'est la mémoire de la mémoire. C'est la mémoire d'une mémoire.

P Sabor: Mais juste pour continuer sur cette question d'évolution, une chose frappante, je trouve, dans la collection, c'est qu'on a organisé la collection non pas selon l'ordre chronologique dans lequel les histoires ont été écrites, mais plutôt selon le temps qui passe; vous arrangez les nouvelles d'une telle façon qu'on ne peut suivre une évolution; s'il y a une évolution, elle est dans le style.

MG: Alors nous parlons d'un livre qui n'a pas été traduit en français parce qu'il est trop gros. Mais j'explique cela pour les francophones, qui ne l'auront pas lu. J'ai placé les nouvelles selon l'époque où elles se situent, c'est-à-dire qu'une nouvelle écrite en 1954 est à côté d'une [nouvelle] écrite trente ans après, mais située en 1954. Je croyais que, pour les lecteurs, ce serait intéressant.

P Sabor: Tout à fait, je suis d'accord.

MG: Ah oui? je croyais que ça ne vous avait pas plu.

P Sabor: Non, non, pas du tout. Je trouve ça très intéressant, mais en même temps j'imagine qu'un critique qui voulait étudier…

MG: Les dates sont à la fin.

P Sabor: Oui c'est vrai. On peut toujours relire de cette façon-là. Au contraire, je trouve que la façon dont c'est arrangé est très agréable.

MG: On m'a dit que je pouvais faire ce que je voulais, alors j'ai fait ça (*rires*).

AW: D'autres questions?

NC: Je voulais peut-être vous demander d'élaborer sur la question de la mémoire, qui est si importante dans vos écrits. Qui est à la fois reconstruction et imagination. Parfois on a l'impression que certains personnages—tout le monde reconstruit, évidemment; ce qu'on voit dans voş nouvelles, c'est que chacun doit reconstruire son passé pour en faire du sens—mais certains personnages chez vous reconstruisent leur passé tout en en mettant de côté de grands pans, pour ne pas avoir à faire face à certaines douleurs.

MG: Je crois que c'est fréquent. Et c'était conscient. Je n'ai jamais connu quelqu'un qui ait dit: maintenant j'oublie exactement ce que j'étais entre 20 et 25 ans. Ce n'est pas possible. Ou j'oublie cet oncle que je n'aimais pas ou j'oublie mon pays natal, que je détestais. Ça ne se fait pas consciemment, mais inconsciemment, et ça ne reste pas. Mais ce n'est pas *mémoire de mémoire*. Je pensais surtout à Montréal et à des nouvelles situées à Montréal, le Montréal généralement de ma jeunesse, de mon enfance, ou de la jeunesse et de l'enfance des autres. Mais je sais comment ça se passait parce que je connaissais les rues, je connaissais les endroits, je connaissais la façon de vivre. Et donc le Montréal que j'ai connu reste. Quand je pense Montréal, je vois le Montréal que j'ai connu. Je ne le vois pas tel qu'il est aujourd'hui. Quand j'arrive, je vois cette autre ville; elle est là, c'est différent, mais pour l'écriture, ça revient toujours au Montréal de mes souvenirs. Au coin des rues St-Denis et Sherbrooke, il y a ce terrain vague, je sais pas si ça fait des années que ce terrain est vague—eh bien là, il y avait une école où j'étais en pension, c'est Saint-Louis-de-Gonzague—et quand j'y pense, si je pense à ce bout de la rue Sherbrooke, je vois cet édifice en pierre; il y faisait un peu sombre, mais c'étaient les couvents de l'époque. Mais c'est ça que j'aurais dans l'esprit. Je vois tout. Je vois les pierres, je vois les arbres, les arbres sont restés d'ailleurs, oui. Et puis, comment on entrait, circulait; c'était comme ça, je vois cela. Mais quand je le vois, je sais que ça fait des années que ça n'existe pas, et ça ne me choque pas. Ça n'existe pas, c'est un terrain vague. Donc il y a une double… C'est ça, *mémoire de mémoire*.

NC: Je me demandais, quand vous retournez à Montréal, est-ce que l'image du Montréal d'aujourd'hui se superpose à l'image que vous aviez du Montréal d'autrefois et ferait que vos souvenirs deviennent plus confus?

MG: Non, non, je n'ai pas de problème parce que je ne l'habite pas, donc c'est resté intact. C'est un peu comme—je ne sais pas s'il vous est arrivé de revoir quelqu'un que vous n'avez pas vu pendant vingt ans. Alors vous voyez tout à fait votre visage, et pendant la conversation, le visage du jeune homme que vous avez connu glisse là-dessus. C'est absolument extraordinaire, et vous le voyez tel qu'il était, et pas tel qu'il est. Mais à chaque fois que vous allez le revoir, vous allez avoir un choc, et après ça s'amoindrit. Est-ce que vous avez eu cette expérience? Quelqu'un l'a eue?

P-ER: C'est le bal de têtes du *Temps retrouvé*. Et pour Montréal, c'est la conclusion de … *Du côté de chez Swann…*

MG: Quand il prend Gilberte pour sa mère.

P-ER: Oui c'est ça, «Vous me prenez pour maman», oui. Et puis pour le terrain vague, c'est la conclusion de *Du Côté de chez Swann*, «car les avenues sont fugitives, hélas, comme les années».

AW: Là ce qui me frappe, c'est qu'en fait, c'est la mémoire, alors que vous avez commencé cette réflexion en disant que les gens reconstruisent le passé par un oubli sélectif.

MG: Ah, ça c'est extraordinaire. Je retourne au Canada tous les ans, mais j'ai le souvenir de la vie de mes amis, je me souviens d'eux jeunes. Et on va me raconter des choses: «Tu te souviens…», mais c'est complètement faux. Mais je ne peux pas dire: «Mais non, votre père était alcoolique» (*rires*). «Qu'est-ce que vous racontez? Ce n'est pas vrai.» Probablement que nous l'avons tous fait, probablement que chaque personne dans cette pièce a reconstruit quelque chose sans s'en rendre compte. Je viens de lire, voilà, quelque chose de Mordecai Richler. On me l'a envoyé du Canada et il écrit sur la mort de son ami Brian Moore, que j'ai connu. Il dit: «C'est Mavis Gallant qui me l'a présenté à Paris». C'est complètement faux. Il était très peu à Paris. Moore venait à Paris, je ne le voyais pas et il avait d'autres choses. Ils n'ont jamais été ici en même temps que moi, et il y a des raisons, d'autres raisons qui auraient empêché cette rencontre: je ne m'entendais pas avec Moore, alors je n'avais pas intérêt à lui présenter qui que ce soit. Et puis Richler était ici, il avait dix-huit, dix-neuf ans. C'est un roman. Dans son esprit, ça doit être vrai, ou il n'aurait jamais publié [cela], mais je pourrais faire un tableau de toutes les raisons pour lesquelles ce n'était pas possible. Mais il doit le croire ou il ne l'aurait pas publié, c'est quelque chose qui a paru il y a quelques semaines, on me l'a envoyé. Jamais, jamais. C'est plein de choses qui n'ont pas eu lieu. Et d'autres choses sur Paris, et je suis sûre que ce n'est pas délibéré, parce qu'il ne prendrait pas ce risque, c'est stupide, tant qu'il y a des témoins encore vivants et vigilants (rires). Mais c'est un exemple de la mémoire reconstruite. Dans son souvenir, en 1951, je le présentais à Brian Moore, qui n'était même pas à Paris.

AW: On dirait que vous restez fascinée par les pouvoirs de reconstruction de l'être humain. Par cette capacité de refaire la réalité comme on voudrait qu'elle soit.

MG: Peut-être, mais pas en théorie. Enfin, je n'ai pas de théorie là-dessus.

P. Sabor: Mais du côté pratique, je trouve que ce que vous venez de nous dire est important, parce qu'il y a beaucoup de monde qui ont lu la même chose. Moi je l'ai lu, l'article dans lequel Mordecai Richler parle de Brian Moore. Et après, on va commencer à faire des liens entre Brian Moore et vous (rires).

MG: Non, je le connaissais, mais on ne s'entendait pas, on était très différents. Je ne peux pas imaginer une situation où j'aurais présenté Moore à ce jeune, à ce très jeune garçon. Oui, mais ça devient une histoire.

Mais écoutez, il y a l'ancienne prison du Cherche-Midi, où il y a maintenant cette chose assez laide. Il y a une plaque où on dit: «il y avait ici une prison où on a fait le premier procès d'Alfred Dreyfus». C'est complètement faux. Il a été fait où se trouve maintenant le boulevard Raspail. On a démoli—c'était un ancien couvent qui a été démoli en 1910 pour faire le boulevard Raspail. J'ai téléphoné à la commission du Vieux-Paris; j'étais très mécontente, et vous savez ce qu'on m'a répondu? «Oh c'est comme ça qu'on fait l'histoire». Alors vous voyez, il y a fiction dans la fiction.

AW: C'est en fait toute la question de l'histoire et de la redécouverte de l'histoire, d'une correction de l'histoire, d'une réévaluation de l'histoire, l'importance de la mémoire pour l'être humain, les choses dont il faudrait se souvenir. Est-ce que c'est là une réflexion pour vous aussi, une réflexion sur les événements? L'histoire, une réflexion historique est présente dans votre—.

MG: Mais je crois que je n'ai pas de réflexion très profonde sur quoi que ce soit. Ce sont des choses qui m'arrivent à l'esprit, c'est autre chose… et qui sont traduites par des faits pour faire une fiction.

AW: Justement, dans la préface de *Home Truths*, on lit cette même idée—et je vais citer Mavis Gallant: "The character I called Linnet Muir is not an exact reflection. I saw her as quite another person, but it would be untrue to say that I invented everything. I can vouch for the city: my Montreal is as accurate as memory can make it. I looked nothing up, feeling that if I made a mistake with the street name, it had to stand. Memory can spell a name wrong and still convey the truth. «*Je suis un mensonge qui dit la vérité*». That was Jean Cocteau. It is not the last word about the writing of fiction, because no last word exists; but it says, briefly and plainly, what I might put with less grace" (xxii).

MG: Je crois que je pourrais écrire ça aujourd'hui, oui. On peut se tromper sur l'orthographe d'une rue ou quelque chose, mais c'est vrai. Ça reste vrai.

AW: Je pense que c'est un excellent mot de la fin, la fiction comme mensonge qui reste vrai; c'est un excellent point de clôture, tout en laissant, comme l'auteure aime le faire dans ses nouvelles, des ambiguïtés, et tout en laissant à l'assistance le plaisir de creuser encore le sens des interventions de nos participants à la table ronde et de Mavis Gallant elle-même. Au nom de toute l'assistance, merci à Jane Koustas, Geneviève Doze, Pierre-Edmond Robert, Nicole Côté, et surtout à Mavis Gallant.

Mavis Gallant

Questions and Answers/Questions et réponses

Participants: *Linda Leith (LL) Moderator / Modératrice, Nicole Côté (NC), Marta Dvorak (MD), Mavis Gallant (MG), Janice Kulyk Keefer (JKK), Jacques Leclaire (JL), Danielle Schaub (DS), Agnès Whitfield (AW).*

LL: Après une telle journée, dédiée aux écrits de Mavis Gallant, ce n'est vraiment pas nécessaire d'introduire Mavis Gallant elle-même. J'aimerais tout de même bien dire que c'est un auteur, un écrivain qui a gagné plusieurs prix, dont le prix du Gouverneur Général du Canada, le prix Molson.

She is an author who has received many prizes, many honours which are richly deserved, and after whom at least one literary prize has been named, The Q-Spell Mavis Gallant prize for non-fiction.

Alors Mavis a peut-être un texte à nous lire pour commencer cette séance de questions. C'est avec un grand plaisir que je laisse la parole à Mavis Gallant.

MG: Si vous avez quelques questions à me poser, je réponds, je réponds à tout (*rires*) et à n'importe quoi. Personne n'aime poser la première question, alors je vais commencer par les réponses, en vous disant que je n'utilise pas d'ordinateur, que j'écris à la main; que je récris ce texte à la machine, comme j'ai toujours fait, et que dans la vie courante je parle le français plus souvent que je ne parle l'anglais. Il y a des jours et des jours où je ne dis pas un mot en anglais, mais l'anglais reste ma langue d'écriture. On ne la choisit pas, c'est elle qui vous choisit. Voilà. J'ai apporté un discours que j'avais fait à la Société des anglicistes de l'enseignement supérieur, à leur trente-quatrième congrès à Valenciennes, en 1994. Ill n'y a pas longtemps qu'on me l'a renvoyé. On a mis cinq ans pour publier (*rires*) le résultat aux Presses Universitaires. Je pensais qu'il y avait—ne craignez rien, je ne vais pas vous lire le discours, car il dure quarante minutes—mais il y avait certaines choses qui répondent un peu à ce que—vous m'entendez? Oui—c'est en anglais, je lisais à des anglicistes et donc ça n'a jamais été traduit en français. Janet Flanner—une grande journaliste, morte maintenant, who was the *New Yorker* correspondent in Paris for fifty years—once reproached me for "living in French," *entre guillemets*, as she put it. She seemed to feel that I had become totally French minded, with a world outlook centred in France, cut away from English speaking readers. (Je crois que ce n'était pas vrai, j'ai continué à écrire en anglais). I did not agree, then, and I still don't. She said of herself that her imaginative life, as she put it, belonged to Paris. She would not contemplate living elsewhere, and in fact she went home to America only after she became very old and couldn't go on living alone in Paris. The difference between us, the difference that led her to tell me that I lived in French, *comme reproche*, was that even in Paris she spoke more English than French, probably owing to the nature of her social life; whereas I spent (I actually spend) days on end without uttering a word in English, except in my mind. I cannot compose in any language but English. If I began to write an excellent French, if it came easily to me to write French at all, and it doesn't —I would lose English as my writing language, but without linking French to imaginative thinking. I would have to move away from France and to an English-speaking environment. It would mean moving away from Paris, and I would not want that at all.

About Madame Whitfield's most interesting discussion of "Across the Bridge," what I want to say is that if a writer of fiction wrote from that point of view, there would be no fiction at all. There is a profound difference between [writing fiction and writing criticism]. I'm not talking about reviewing, but criticism, authentic academic criticism, which is necessary for research. But the raw material of fiction has come from another source, so that criticism is almost impossible for the author to follow. The critic might as well be writing it in Swahili as any other exotic language. There is a glass wall between the writer and the critic. I am talking about criticism, not reviewing. Someone who has to review a book once a week can just say what it's about and what he or she thinks of it. It is done as a service to readers, to those who may or may not buy the book. That's something else. For serious critics, the problem is that no matter how much is revealed in the text, the sources of fiction remain invisible. I think that only critics who also write fiction understand that. I often wonder how it is that they don't become schizophrenic, what with the fiction that comes from one source within them and the criticism, which necessarily comes from without. They are inside and outside all at once. There is a great difference between those who read purely for pleasure, the ideal audience, and those who read as a professional duty. A house described in fiction will be reconstructed for any kind of reader as the house he may have lived in as a child (or she, just to make it clear). Obviously, for the critic and theorist, a subjective image is not enough. He (and when I say "he", I mean he-or-she) wants the image or the element that shaped the original image for the writer. It is his business to do away with words and sentences in order to discover what produced them, even though words are the best the writer can offer. In fact, they are all that can be offered. I don't know if this is clear; I hope so.

A reviewer writing in a magazine or literary journal has limited time, not too much space, and a great number of things to read, on which to make an instant judgement. It is on his opinion that readers will decide if the book is worth reading. The researcher is trying to discover something that never occurred to the author. He will find it. His future may depend on finding it. It may be entirely in his own imagination, as characters and places described are part of the author's. Presented with the discovery, the author will neither recognize nor understand it. It will make no sense, not even as an idea. In other words, there is no meeting. That is what I think and feel. If anybody wants to discuss this, I'd be delighted.

LL: Est-ce qu'il y a un commentaire là-dessus?

DS: Oui. You take away our *raison d'être*.

MG: Not at all. I said that I understand the need for research.

DS: But this is the constant conflict between the writer and the critic, [the writer] who says: well, I'm the writer, you're the critic.

MG: No, it is not a conflict. All I am saying is that what to the critic is raw material to the writer is the culmination. It is as smooth as this table top. You can't do anything to it except scratch the surface, or try to reassess it completely. Is this wood? Is this varnish? All this is as alien as another language to the person who produced it. But I am not criticizing the critic!

DS: I didn't take it as criticism. We've had these conversations before but, in a way, by putting it the way you put it, it's as if, well, why do we have to do that? Why do we feel the need to go into—?

MG: Non pas du tout. I wouldn't have given this talk to a group of teachers, whose business it is to teach, not to break down a text. But I thought it was important to say.

DS: But no, that's exactly the way you feel, and I think it's important for you to say. And I think it's true that the writers, hearing what other people have to say about what they've written, may feel alienated because it's no longer theirs. It becomes somebody else's. It's changed. It's meddled with, in some ways, because the person is trying to show how it functions, and so I can understand why you're saying it.

LL: As a critic of Mavis Gallant, you're not writing for Mavis. You're writing for a different readership altogether. You're speaking to a different audience. When, as in this kind of session today, the author herself is present, you actually have a conjunction of these two ways of looking at the same material. As a novelist myself and a critic, I find that I agreed completely with what Mavis has said; I don't know what Janice would think. I mean they are very different ways of looking at the material.

JKK: I think there are different kinds of criticisms, and that research-oriented criticism, which tries to find out the shape of a writer's oeuvre or the influences upon it, and relates it to other literary movements and the place of the writer and her epoch or whatever, is one kind of criticism; but I think there is another kind, that allows a greater attentiveness to the writing, that allows the reader to participate in some way or to experience just how language is used and how meaning is shaped, and to me, that's one of the pleasures of doing a critical—well what do you call it—an attentive reading of a text. It is one of the great pleasures of dealing with Mavis Gallant's work that it is so rich, that there is so much to attend to. And critically attentive reading doesn't necessarily ask: "what exactly did you mean there?" or: "is this influenced by that?" but rather can become a way of conversing with the writers about characters and situations in fiction, and their resonances with the reader's own thoughts and experiences. I wonder whether that also would be a "foreign language" to the writer, or whether it can give her a sense of connection to those who are reading for a variety of pleasures, including the pleasure of understanding how a story comes to be shaped and the way in which it represents the world we share with the writer.

MG: I want to make it plain, again, that I'm not making light of work of this kind. Even though the end result might be of works having been put through a wringer. Not long ago—je vous lis un peu, excusez-moi, je ne l'ai pas en français, ce texte—not long ago, I had a letter from a teacher in an American university, working on a doctoral thesis on Henry James. He is using as part of his material an early novel of mine and some of my stories. It is the kind of request for information that must be answered. Because I am aware of that, I answer everything, and I try to be as helpful as I can; even though I think that this man and I are merely floating in the same space with no chance of ever touching. Or are we on different escalators? Or is one going up and the other down, and the most we can do is wave as we pass? May I please insist again that work he intends to use for such a serious purpose was intended to be read only for pleasure (*laughs*). And that I believe in the truth of Samuel Johnson's dictum: "What is read as a task will do you no good." I believe it so strongly that I copied it and kept it on my desk in case I am ever tempted to fall into the trap of reading, not for enjoyment, but as forced labour. For the awful further truth is that, as well as fiction, I do write literary articles, essays, and reviews, usually on French authors. My awareness that I am quite limited and could never consider doing serious research, even if I had a taste for it, is what compels me to lend people who are doing it all the help I can. Even if the aim and purpose of the idea strikes me as beside the point, however; even when boosted by due respect, how can the writer of fiction respond: "Here is a teacher whose thesis concerns Henry James?" I might think, but this is what he says: "The subject of my dissertation involves intertext," which seems to me to mean the study of scripture. I do not understand what he wants. He says he wants to (quote) "dispense with the issues of influence" and (more quote) "view literature as a form of dialogue between authors." To illustrate his thesis, he is proposing to use this novel and he asks (quote): "Was *A Fairly Good Time* written as a reply to James's *Portrait of a Lady*?" One's first reaction, that the very proposition makes no sense, is overtaken by the realization it makes sense to *him*. We are simply on different escalators moving in different directions. He's assuming that the kernel of a novel, which is for me a vivid image, is from the same source as the argument of a thesis. It would never have entered my head to write a novelist's reply to another novel, let alone to a masterwork of the age. I'll stop now, because some of the people here don't understand English.

AW: I'll ask a question then. Nonetheless, you use…

MG: Est-ce que je peux répondre en français? Il y a trois ou quatre personnes ici qui ne comprennent pas l'anglais, alors…

AW: Oui bien sûr. Je vais poser la question en français: Vous évoquez quand même cette image d'être dans—je ne sais pas s'il faudrait dire—le fleuve ou la rivière de la fiction, de l'écriture.

MG: Mais ce n'était pas une image pour moi: *c'est* le fleuve.

AW: Oui, donc c'est le fleuve. Bon, à ce moment-là, vous êtes là comme une cuillerée d'eau dans cette immensité de l'écriture. Comment vous sentez-vous au moment d'écrire? Vous êtes chez vous en écrivant. Vous êtes chez vous dans ce mouvement.

MG: Vous parlez de l'acte d'écrire? "Across the Bridge"? C'est justement la nouvelle dont vous parlez. J'étais en train de la terminer. J'étais vraiment dedans; et je suis sortie dans la rue et pendant une seconde—si cela avait duré plus longtemps, j'aurais pris rendez-vous avec un psychiatre—j'étais étonnée de voir que les gens n'étaient pas habillés à la manière de 1950, et que les voitures, enfin, que les coupes de cheveux étaient bien de 1993. En écrivant une fiction, on est dans ce que j'appelle "The Glass House of Fiction"—«La maison de verre de la fiction»: on est dedans. Et forcément, quelqu'un qui observe du dehors mettra ses mains dessus, mais de l'extérieur. À l'intérieur le climat est tout autre. De l'extérieur,vous voyez mais vous ne le sentez pas. Vous faites partie d'un autre climat. Est-ce que ce n'est pas ça aussi pour toi? Ça pourrait t'arriver de te demander pourquoi on n'est pas habillés d'une autre façon, comme les personnages qui nous occupent et nous préoccupent? (*Réponse incompréhensible*). C'est parce que c'est une romancière de mes amies.

LL: Je crois que pour un écrivain comme Mavis Gallant, qui est surtout un écrivain de nouvelles, il faut chercher l'image qui a fait naître la nouvelle, parce que c'est très souvent une image. Vous êtes saisie par une image et ensuite projetée dans le temps, et tout suit. Si les critiques, enfin, ne peuvent pas se mettre un petit peu dans l'ambiance et comprendre l'image initiale, c'est beaucoup plus difficile.

MG: L'image du début est enfermée dedans. Mais parfois, avant la fin, on la rejette. C'est comme un film qu'on est en train de monter. Il y a des coupures.

JL: Je pense qu'effectivement il est parfois surprenant pour un écrivain d'entendre ce qu'on dit de son oeuvre. Le problème, c'est que la critique arrive toujours après, alors qu'au fond les critiques souvent ont la tentation d'essayer de comprendre comment se crée une oeuvre d'art; et c'est la chose qui est peut-être la plus difficile à approcher. Je pense qu'au départ il y a hommage du critique à l'écrivain, et que le critique, dans le meilleur des cas, se trouve un peu dans la position du chef d'orchestre, qui va donner une interprétation d'une oeuvre, qui sera en partie une création, mais qui a quand même le mérite, me semble-t-il, d'aider l'accès à l'oeuvre. (*Partie du discours perdue*). Ce qui souligne l'importance de l'oeuvre. C'est peut-être présomptueux de le dire, mais je pense que vis-à-vis de l'écrivain, c'est très important qu'il y ait une quantité de critiques de qualité qui soient écrites sur son oeuvre. Mais il ne faut surtout pas que cette critique influence l'écrivain.

MG: J'allais dire: est-ce que vous dites que c'est important pour l'écrivain d'avoir cette critique, ou pour les lecteurs? C'est autre chose. Je ne sais pas, la plupart d'entre nous ont lu par amour, sans jamais…

MD: Est-ce que vous pouvez parler des rapports entre la peinture et l'écriture? Je sais que vous êtes passionnée par la peinture, et je me demande si vous trouvez des liens entre les deux activités? Qu'est-ce que les tableaux vous donnent en tant qu'amateur?

MG: Ce n'est pas quelque chose de défini; je regarde la peinture depuis que je suis enfant. C'est une partie de ma vie comme la musique, mais je ne sais pas lire une partition. Mon père était peintre amateur. Un de mes premiers souvenirs est de mon père me tenant dans ses bras pour me montrer un tableau, une scène de neige, au Musée des Beaux-Arts. Il y avait de la neige, il y avait des arbres et il y avait les ombres et il m'a dit: «tu vois, la neige n'est pas blanche, elle est bleue, elle est grise, elle est mauve.» Ça m'est toujours resté. Je crois que ces choses sont dans la profondeur de la mémoire et reviennent, tout au long de la vie. Excusez-moi, je m'explique mal.

NC: Je sais que vous vous intéressez beaucoup à la musique et je me demandais, puisque vous en avez glissé un mot, si vous ne vouliez pas…

MG: Non, je ne peux pas lire une partition. Je vous ai dit, je ne joue pas d'instrument de musique, mais c'est la même chose, j'ai écouté [de la musique] toute ma vie. Un poème, tiré d'un nouveau livre de Derek Walcott, a été publié dans le *Times Literary Supplement*, à Londres, il y a deux ou trois semaines. Et tout ce livre de poésie est en rapport avec un seul tableau. Ça va vous intéresser.

MD: Puisqu'on a parlé d'art, d'images et de musique, et chez vous, je crois, quand vous écrivez, l'image est très importante, et la voix aussi. Alors qu'est-ce qui prime finalement? Par quoi commencez-vous? Par l'image, et ensuite vous travaillez la voix, ou est-ce la voix qui vient d'abord?

MG: Non c'est une image, mais chaque écrivain est différent. Je ne crois pas que la fiction prenne le même départ pour chacun, ni pour les mêmes raisons. Je ne peux que parler de moi. J'ai beaucoup d'amis écrivains, et chacun entre dans un nouveau travail par une autre porte. Pour moi, c'est une image fixe qui me vient à l'esprit, je ne sais pas d'où, évidemment ça vient de moi, mais je ne sais pas par quel chemin. Ce sont des gens dans une situation, comme dans un film qui s'arrête. Et je les vois et je sais qui ils sont. Je sais qui ils sont, je sais leurs noms, mais je peux changer les noms parfois.

MD: Mais est-ce que la voix vient aussi à ce moment-là, ou est-ce qu'il faut la travailler?

MG: Les personnages arrivent. Au départ, l'image sera silencieuse. Et puis, le film se met en route, si vous voulez, et chacun parle et bouge avec sa voix, son accent, son vocabulaire. L'accent est important. S'ils parlent en français, en anglais, ils ont un accent. Ils ont des professions. Ils ont des inquiétudes. Tout commence à se dénouer. Cette image se dénoue et je commence à écrire. Ce qui m'est venu tout de suite dans "Across the Bridge" était la mère et sa fille traversant le pont de la Concorde, la mère portant le sac avec les invitations au mariage qui seront jetées à la Seine. Tout ça était très clair au départ. Je crois que Mme Whitfield s'est trompée sur les raisons qui font que la fille retraverse le pont, à la fin. C'est simplement qu'elle retourne chez ses parents, pour le moment. Mais c'est une coïncidence; ce qui est intéressant, c'est que je ne me suis jamais rendu compte, avant de l'entendre dire: «elle ne retraverse pas le pont;» et je pensais: oui oui oui, elle l'a fait, elle retourne rive droite, qui est la bourgeoisie, *etc*. Mais c'est une coïncidence et je n'avais jamais, dans mon esprit, pensé: rive gauche, rive droite; non, non, ça c'est fait comme cela. Mais ça, traverser le pont avec sa mère, qui est assez dirigeante, assez directive, et lui tenir tête et dire: je ne veux pas épouser ce garçon, et la mère qui prend les invitations et «flac,» et qui dit: «si c'est comme ça». Elles tombent à l'eau et elles ont ce mouvement de se séparer à la surface de l'eau, mais ce n'est que le mouvement d'objets jetés à l'eau, qui flottent. Ce n'est pas quelque chose qui ait une signification. Ça se fait tout naturellement. N'importe quoi jeté à l'eau, vous verrez, fera «flac.»J'ai trouvé intéressante l'idée des deux ponts. Je n'avais jamais pensé à ça. Mais si je me mettais à y penser, si je commençais à écrire de cette façon, ce serait illisible. C'est un des torts des jeunes écrivains français aujourd'hui: ils commencent par la théorie. Ils commencent par une théorie, et cela devient illisible et parfois prétentieux.

LL: Je crois que vous procédez un peu comme un peintre, par touches, parce que vous évoquez toute une période par une petite touche, un détail de la façon dont on est habillé ou un accent, ou enfin un petit peu comme un peintre sur une toile, et c'est cela qu'on trouve dans les meilleures nouvelles, et qu'on ne trouve pas toujours dans un long roman où vous êtes obligé d'utiliser une certaine économie de moyens, comme ça.

MG: J'ai vu mon père peindre. Mais ce sont de lointains souvenirs. J'étais petite.

Bibliography

Atwood, Margaret. *The Handmaid's Tale*. Toronto: McClelland and Stewart, 1985.

Auden, W.H. *Selected Poems*. New York: Vintage, 1979.

Barthes, Roland. "La Bruyère." *Essais critiques*. Paris: Seuil (Collection Tel Quel), 1964.

Besner, Neil K. "A Broken Dialogue: History and Memory in Mavis Gallant's Short Fiction." *Essays on Canadian Writing*, 33 (Fall 1986): 88–99.

————. *The Light of Imagination: Mavis Gallant's Fiction*. Vancouver: University of British Columbia Press, 1988.

————. "Rereading the 'Moslem Wife': Irony in the Light of Imagination." Unpublished paper presented at the ACSUS Congress, Boston, November 1991.

Blanchot, Maurice. *The Infinite Conversation*. Trans. Susan Hanson. Minneapolis: University of Minnesota Press,1993.

Blodgett, E. D. "Heresy and the Other Arts: A Measure of Mavis Gallant's Fiction." *Essays on Canadian Writing* 42 (Winter 1990) [special Gallant issue]: 1–8.

Borges, Jorge Luis. *Fictions*. Trans. Alastair Reid. London: Calder and Boyars, 1965.

Buckler, Ernest. *Buckler Manuscript Collection*, Thomas Fisher Rare Book Library, University of Toronto, Toronto.

Cooper, J. C. *Symbolic and Mythological Animals*. London: Aquarian, 1992.

de Man, Paul. *Blindness and Insight: Essays in the Rhetoric of Contemporary Criticism*. 2nd ed. Minneapolis: University of Minnesota Press, 1983.

Derrida, Jacques. "Living On: Border Lines." In *Deconstruction and Criticism*, ed. Harold Bloom *et al.*New York: Continuum, 1984, pp.75–176.

———— *Marges de la philosophie*. Paris: Minuit, 1972.

———— and Maurizio Ferraris. *A Taste for the Secret*, ed.Giacomo Donis and David Webb. Trans. Giacomo Donis. Cambridge: Polity, 2001.

de Vries, Ad. *Dictionary of Symbols and Imagery*. Amsterdam and London: North-Holland Publishing Company, 1974.

Dupriez, Bernard. *A Dictionary of Literary Devices: Gradus, A–Z*. Trans. and adapted by Albert W. Halsall. Toronto and Buffalo: University of Toronto Press, 1991.

Foucault, Michel. *Les Mots et les choses*. Paris: Gallimard, 1966.

Gallant, Mavis. *De l'autre côté du pont*. Trans. Geneviève Doze. Paris: Fayard, 1994.

————. *From the Fifteenth District: A Novella and Eight Short Stories*. New York: Random House, 1979; rpt. Toronto: Macmillan, 1979.

————. *Home Truths*. Toronto: Stoddart, 1992.

————. *The Other Paris: Stories*. Boston: Houghton Mifflin, 1956; rpt. Toronto: Macmillan, 1986.

————. *The Paris Notebooks. Essays and Reviews by Mavis Gallant*. Toronto: Macmillan, 1968 and 1986.

————. *Rue de Lille*. Trans. Pierre-Edmond Robert. Paris: Editions Tierce, 1988.

————. *The Selected Stories of Mavis Gallant*. Toronto: McClelland and Stewart, 1996.

————. "What Is Style?" *Canadian Forum*, September 1982.

Geddes, Gary, ed. *Twentieth-Century Poetry and Poetics*. 4th ed. Toronto: Oxford University Press, 1995.

Girard, Anne-Marie, and Claude Pamela Valette. "Entretien avec Mavis Gallant." *Les Cahiers de la nouvelle*, 2 (January 1984): 79–94.

Godard, Barbara. "Modalities of the Edge: Towards a Semiotics of Irony: The Case of Mavis Gallant." *Essays on Canadian Writing* 42 (Winter 1990) [special Gallant issue]: 72–101.

Hancock, Geoff. "An Interview with Mavis Gallant." *Canadian Fiction Magazine* 28 (1978) [special Gallant issue]: 19–67; rpt. in Hancock's *Canadian Writers at Work* (Toronto: Oxford University Press, 1987).

Hatch, Ronald. "The Three Stages of Mavis Gallant's Short Fiction." *Canadian Fiction Magazine* 28 (1978) [special Gallant issue]: 92–114.

Hutcheon, Linda ."Introduction." *Double-Talking: Essays on Verbal and Visual Ironies in Contemporary Canadian Art and Literature*. Ed. Linda Hutcheon. Toronto: ECW Press, 1992.

————. "The Power of Postmodern Irony." In *Genre, Trope, Gender: Critical Essays*, ed. Barry Rutland (Ottawa: Carleton University Press, 1992).

————. *Splitting Images: Contemporary Canadian Ironies*. Toronto: Oxford University Press, 1991.

Jewison, Donald. "Speaking of Mirrors: Imagery and Narration in Two Novellas by Mavis Gallant." *Studies in Canadian Literature* 10, 1–2 (1985): 100–2.

Keefer, Janice Kulyk. "Bridges and Chasms: Multiculturalism and Mavis Gallant's 'Virus X.'" *World Literature Written in English*, 31.2 (1991): 100–11.

————. *Reading Mavis Gallant*. Oxford: Oxford University Press, 1989.

Kurosawa, Akira. *Rashomon*. Japan, 1950: 90 m.

LaCapra, Dominick. *History, Politics, and the Novel*. Ithaca: Cornell University Press, 1987.

Le Guern, Michel. *Sémantique de la métaphore et de la métonymie*. Paris: Larousse, 1973.

Lichtheim, George. *Europe in the Twentieth Century*. London: Cardinal, 1974.

Merler, Grazia. *Mavis Gallant: Narrative Patterns and Devices*. Ottawa: Tecumseh Press, 1978.

Morier, Henri. *Dictionnaire de Poétique et de Rhétorique*. Paris: Presses Universitaires de France, 1961.

Muecke, D.C. *Irony*. London: Methuen, 1970.

————. *Irony and the Ironic*. London: Methuen, 1982.

O'Donnel, Maureen. "Lettres d'introduction." *Financial Post*, 11 May 1996, pp. 22–3.

Poore, Charles. "Books of 'The Times': Mavis Gallant's Stories of Exiles and their Hearth."*The New York Times*, 16 April 1964, p. 3.

Ricoeur, Paul. *La Métaphore vive*. Paris: Seuil, 1975.

Siemerling, Winfried. "Perception, Memory, Irony: Mavis Gallant Greets Proust and Flaubert." *Essays on Canadian Writing* 42 (Winter 1990) [special Gallant issue]: 131–53.

Smythe, Karen. *Figuring Grief: Gallant, Munro and the Poetics of Elegy*. Montreal and Kingston: McGill-Queen's University Press, 1992.

Van Gunsteren, Julia. *Katherine Mansfield and Literary Impressionism*. Amsterdam: Rodopi, 1990.

Van Spanckeren, Kathryn, and Jan G. Castro, eds. *Margaret Atwood: Vision and Forms*. Carbondale: Southern Illinois University Press,1988.

Woodsworth, Judith. "Writers and their Translators: the Case of Mavis Gallant." *Traduction, Terminologie, Rédaction*, 1 (1988): 47–57.

Yeats, W.B. *Selected Poetry*, ed. Timothy Webb. London: Penguin, 1991.

Zand, Nicole. "Mavis Gallant, Québécoise de langue anglaise." *Le Monde*, 13 Novembre 1987, p. 24.

Contributors

Nicole Côté teaches Quebec literature and literary translation at the University of Regina. She has published in *Meta*, *TTR*, *Protée* and the *University of Toronto Quarterly*, mainly on Canadian and Québec short stories. She has translated several short story writers, including Mavis Gallant, and has edited *Nouvelles du Canada anglais*.

Geneviève Doze grew up in England and France. Immersed in two cultures, she naturally moved on to literary translation. Her first book translation was Don Talyesva's *Sun Chief* (*Soleil Hopi*). She taught English at school and at university (Brazzaville, Rabat, Lille, Aix-en-Provence), until retirement. Mavis Gallant, Christina Garcia, Elizabeth Jolley, Alice Munro, Elizabeth Spencer, Elizabeth Taylor and Joy Williams are among the authors she has translated. She is currently translating two novels: J.G. Farrell's *The Singapore Grip* and Yvonne Vera's *Butterfly Burning*.

Marta Dvorak teaches Canadian and Commonwealth Literature at the Sorbonne Nouvelle. She has edited books on subjects ranging from Canadian cinema, bilingualism and multiculturalism, to biographical production and Margaret Atwood. She won the Margaret Atwood Society Best Article Award (1999) and contributed to *Margaret Atwood, The Handmaid's Tale: The Power Game*, which won the Society's Best Book Award. She is the author of *Ernest Buckler: Rediscovery and Reassessment* and is currently editing a selection of Buckler's short fiction and a book on Nancy Huston.

Jane Koustas is Professor of French at Brock University, Ontario, where she also directs the Centre for Canadian Studies. Her research interests lie primarily in the fields of Quebec theatre, translation and theatre translation. She has published in *Meta*, *TTR*, and the *University of Toronto Quarterly*, and is co-editor of a book on Robert Lepage.

Janice Kulyk Keefer teaches at the University of Guelph, Ontario. The author of short stories, novels, poetry, and critical studies, including *Reading Mavis Gallant* (1989), she has won numerous awards, including the CBC Radio Literary Competition for fiction, the Canadian Authors' Association award for poetry, and the Marian Engel award. She has also been short-listed for the Governor General's Award for non-fiction and for fiction. She is currently working on a novel dealing with Katherine Mansfield.

Linda Leith's first novel, *Birds of Passage* (1993), was serialized on the CBC radio programme "Between the Covers" and favourably reviewed in the *Times Literary Supplement*, the *Budapest Sun*, and across Canada. Her second novel, *The Tragedy Queen*, appeared in 1995, and she is the author of a non-fiction study, *Introducing Hugh MacLennan's Two Solitudes* (1990). She was publisher and editor of *Matrix* (1988–95) and editor of *Telling Differences: New English Fiction in Quebec* (1989). She is director of the Blue Metropolis International Literary Festival in Montreal.

Pierre-Edmond Robert is Professor of French and Head of "Didactique du français, langue étrangère" at Université de Paris III-Sorbonne nouvelle. He has published widely on Proust, L.-F. Céline and Eugène Dabit. He has translated several of Mavis Gallant's short stories and short-story collections, including "Les Vieux Amis" ("The Old Friends"), 1988, *Les Quatres Saisons* (*From the Fifteenth District*), 1989, "Le Royaume des cieux" ("Kingdom Come"), 1990, and *Rue de Lille* (*Overhead in a Balloon*), 1993. He is also the author of three short-story collections and two novels.

Peter Sabor, Professor of English literature at Université Laval, Quebec, is the author of books on and editions of several eighteenth-century British novelists, including Samuel Richardson, Sarah Fielding, John Cleland, Horace Walpole, Frances Burney, and Jane Austen. He is a longstanding admirer of the luminous short stories of Mavis Gallant.

Danielle Schaub teaches in the English Department of Oranim, Israel. She has published numerous articles on Canadian literature, particularly on women writers. She has co-edited *Precarious Present / Promising Future?*

Ethnicity and Identities in Canadian Literature (1996), published *Mavis Gallant* (1998), edited *Mapping Canadian Cultural Space: Essays on Canadian Literature* (2000), and is co-editing a collection of essays on Identity, Community, Nation. She has covered festivals of writers since 1998 and exhibited her photographs of Canadian writers in several countries.

Agnès Whitfield is Professor of Translation at York University, Ontario. She is the author or editor of several books on contemporary Quebec and French-Canadian literature, as well as three volumes of poetry, including *Si les sirènes ne chantaient plus* (2001).

Index